DRIVING G
BRIT.

SUFFOLK

Patricia G. Dalton

LITTLE HILLS PRESS

First Edition, September 1996

Photographs by author
Illustrations by Victoria Schmorl
Cover by NBDesign
Maps drawn by MAPgraphics
Printed in Hong Kong by Magnum International Printing Co Ltd

ISBN 1 86315 094 3

Little Hills Press
Regent House
37-43 Alexander Street
Crows Nest NSW 2065
Australia

Front Cover: The Four Horse Shoes, Thornham Magna.
Back Cover: Flatford Mill, Suffolk.

All distances mentioned in this book are in miles, to correspond with local signposts.
1 mile = 1.6km.

CONTENTS

ACKNOWLEDGEMENTS

In England

Lindsay Want of the East Anglia Tourist Board, Hadleigh, Suffolk.

Tourist Information Centre - Bury St Edmunds
Tourist Information Centre - Lavenham

Geoff & Jose Booker, "Glenham", Playford, Ipswich. Thank you for your warm and very friendly welcome to Suffolk. Geoff remember this:
"Happy to meet, sorry to part
Happy to meet again, happy have we met,
Happy may we part and happy to meet again"

Budget Rent-a-Car, who supplied a wonderful Ford Mondeo, and for the most efficient service and invaluable information received. A special thanks to the team at Dulwich.

In Australia

Catherine Thomas. Without your valued friendship, support, and typing some of my research notes this book would not look as well presented as it does.

Dr John Farmer. Thank you John for all the support and kindness shown in getting me through a difficult time and for always being there when I needed you.

Dr Peter Roberts. Peter (my wonderful chiropractor) without you this series of books would not have been possible. Thank you for all the tireless hours you put in to getting me back on my feet again.

Julian Tumath. Well we did it! Tours 1-17 were made very easy with your navigational skills. I am sure you will remember Eye and Newmarket with fond memories.

Lastly, to my sons Anthony and Alastair, thank you for the love and support you have given me all these years. The East Anglian series of books are dedicated to you both. A special thanks to my wonderful daughter-in-law Jennifer for all the time spent deciphering tapes and typing notes.

INTRODUCTION

East Anglia is made up of the delightful counties of: Suffolk, Norfolk, Essex and Cambridgeshire. Bedfordshire is sometimes included with East Anglia, depending on which maps and books you read.

A fascinating area where a warm welcome awaits you from the people of East Anglia. I take this opportunity to thank all the wonderful, friendly people I had the pleasure of meeting on my travels, without you all these books would not be the font of information they are.

When I decided to go on holiday to England and not knowing where to visit, I bought the usual travel guides. I don't know how other travellers managed to tour the villages and countryside, but I found it extremely difficult trying to plan a holiday and see places of interest when the majority of information was shown only in town/city alphabetical order.

The following tours are set out in such a way that travellers can start in a large county town and then travel through the countryside using lanes, smaller arterial roads and by-ways to discover the real country villages.

The contents index shows places of interest to see, and are numbered to correspond with the appropriate tour. Sports and recreation activities are also listed as are hospitals, police stations and information centres. Also included are market days and early closing days, it is very frustrating to arrive in a town to find that shops are either closed or that the town centre has become a market place, is a hive of activity and parking is a problem.

I hope you enjoy the tours you take, the scenery throughout the year is forever changing and it is well worth visiting the out of the way villages with their special places of interest.

The pubs are truly delightful and meals are very reasonable in all the places mentioned in this book. Accommodation is of course very plentiful with Bed & Breakfast homes being very popular.
If you are going to tour a particular county it may be more practical and economical to rent a self catering cottage or apartment. The listed B&B and self catering accommodation have been either visited by myself or recommended by the British Tourist Authority. Prices quoted are correct at the time of printing and properties should be contacted to ensure availability and changes in rates.

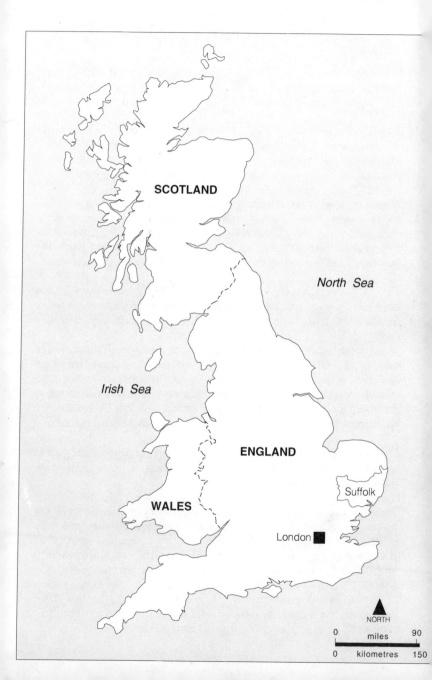

SUMMARY OF TOURS

Tour 1 - Ipswich

Tour 2 - Ipswich Country Tour
Hintlesham, Hadleigh, Kersey, Lindsey, Monks Eleigh, Brent Eleigh, Lavenham, Acton, Great Waldingfield, Newton Green, Polstead, Raydon, Holton St Mary, Ipswich

Tour 3 - Ipswich to Aldeburgh
Martlesham, Woodbridge, Melton, Butley, Chillesford, Orford, Tunstall, Snape, Aldeburgh, Thorpeness, Aldringham, Leiston, Sizewell, Theberton, Yoxford, Sibton, Peasenhall, Dennington, Saxtead Green, Earl Soham, Brandeston, Cretingham, Framsden, Helmingham, Otley, Ashbocking, Witnesham, Tuddenham, Playford, Ipswich

Tour 4 - Ipswich to Easton and Framlingham
Great Bealings, Grundisburgh, Clopton, Easton, Letheringham, Hoo, Kettleburgh, Framlingham, Rendham, Wickham Market, Pettistree, Ipswich

Tour 5 - Ipswich to Lowestoft
Little Glemham, Blythburgh, South Cove, Covehithe, Wrentham, Kessingland, Pakefield, Lowestoft, Corton, Hopton-on-Sea, Gorleston-on-Sea, Fritton, Herringfleet, Somerleyton, Blundeston, Oulton, Carlton Colville, Barnby, Worlingham, Beccles, Shadingfield, Brampton, Stoven, Uggeshall, Holton St Peter, Halesworth, Bramfield, Ipswich

Tour 6 - Ipswich Country Villages
Great Blakenham, Needham Market, Stowupland, Forward Green, Middlewood Green, Mendlesham Green, Mendlesham, Thwaite, Thorndon, Rishangles, Bedingfield, Wilby, Laxfield, Cratfield, Huntingfield, Heveningham, Ubbeston Green, Brundish, Dennington, Saxtead, Monk Soham, Kenton, Debenham, Winston, Pettaugh, Stonham Aspal, Earl Stonham, Coddenham, Claydon, Barham, Henley, Westerfield, Ipswich

Tour 7 - Ipswich to Felixstowe
Martlesham Heath, Waldringfield, Newbourn, Kirton, Felixstowe, Trimley St Mary, Trimley St Martin, Levington, Nacton, Freston, Woolverstone, Chelmondiston, Pin Mill, Shotley, Shotley Gate, Erwarton, Harkstead, Holbrook, Stutton, Alton Waters, Tattingstone, Tattingstone White Horse, Ipswich

Tour 8 - Ipswich to Constable Country
Higham, Thorington Street, Stoke-by-Nayland, Nayland, Great Hokesley, Boxted, Stratford St Mary, Dedham, Flatford, East Bergholt, Brantham, Ipswich

Tour 9 - Ipswich to Southwold
Little Glemham, Saxmundham, Kelsale, Westleton, Dunwich, Dunwich Forest, Walberswick, Blythburgh, Southwold, Reydon, Wangford, Blythburgh, Thorington, Bramfield, Walpole, Sibton, Peasenhall, Bruisyard, Cransford, North Green, Parham, Hacheston, Ipswich

Tour 10 - Ipswich to Bungay
Earl Stonham, Mickfield, Wetheringsett, Stoke Ash, Eye, Hoxne, Cross Street, Heckfield Green, Denham, Horham, Stradbroke, Fressingfield, Weybread, Withersdale Street, Metfield, St Margaret South Elmham, All Saints South Elmham, Rumburgh, Wissett, Spexhall, Ilketshall St Lawrence, Mettingham, Bungay, Earsham, Flixton, Homersfield, Mendham, Redenhall, Needham, Brockdish, Ipswich

Tour 11 - Ipswich to Bury St Edmunds
Chantry, Sproughton, Little Blakenham, Somersham, Offton, Nedging Tye, Bildeston, Hitcham, Cross Green, High Street Green, Great Finborough, Stowmarket, Onehouse, Harleston, Woolpit, Elmswell, Great Ashfield, Hunston, Stowlangtoft, Pakenham, Thurston, Bury St Edmunds

Tour 12 - Bury St Edmunds

Tour 13 - Bury St Edmunds to Clare & Haverhill
Horringer, Whepstead, Brockley Green, Hartest, Boxted, Long Melford, Cavendish, Clare, Stoke-by-Clare, Sturmer, Kedington, Haverhill, Withersfield, Great & Little Thurlow, Wickham Street, Chedburgh, Bury St Edmunds

Tour 14 - Bury St Edmunds to Newmarket
Kentford, Newmarket, Moulton, Gazeley, Dalham, Lidgate, Thorns, Wickhambrook, Wickham Street, Chedburgh, Chevington, Great & Little Saxham, Bury St Edmunds

Tour 15 - Bury St Edmunds to Grimes Graves
Fornham St Martin, Hengrave, Flempton, Lackford, Icklingham, Mildenhall, Brandon, Grimes Graves, Thetford Forest, Mundford, Thetford, Elveden, West Stow, Bury St Edmunds

Tour 16 - Bury St Edmunds to Scole
Haughley, Wetherden, Haughley Green, Earl's Green,
Wyverstone Street, Wyverstone, Bacton, Cotton, Finningham,
Wickham Street, Thornham Magna/Thornham Parva, Mellis,
Yaxley, Eye, Brome, Brome Street, Oakley, Scole, Palgrave,
Wortham, Botesdale, Rickinghall, Wattisfield, Walsham-le-Willows,
Stanton, Ixworth, Great Barton, Bury St Edmunds

Tour 17 - Bury St Edmunds to Sudbury & Country Trail
Little Welnetham, Bradfield St Clare, Great Green, Cockfield,
Alpheton, Bridge Street, Sudbury, Bures, Assington, Bury St
Edmunds

TOUR 1

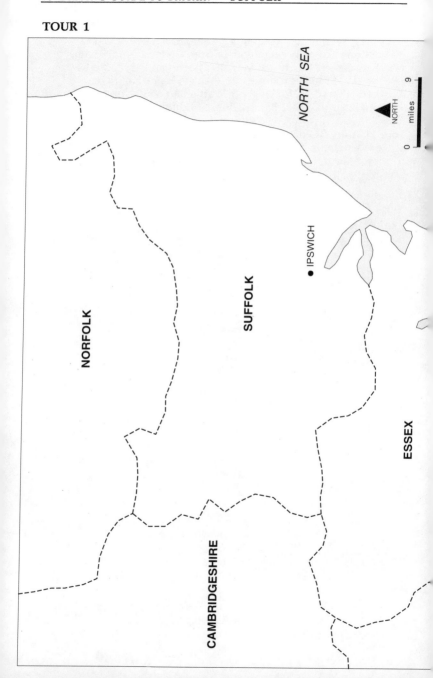

TOURS

Tour 1 - Ipswich

Ipswich

The county town lies on the river Orwell and it was here that Cardinal Wolsey was born about 1475. In 1528 he founded a college in the town, but all that remains is the red-brick gateway in College Street.

Charles Dickens once stayed in the pub *The Great White Horse*, which provided him with a setting for *Pickwick Papers*.

Location: On the A12, 12 miles north-west of Felixstowe.

Information Centre: St Stephen's Church, St Stephen's Lane.

Hospital: Ipswich Hospital, Heath Road.

Police: Civic Drive.

Market Days: Tuesday, Friday & Saturday.

Early Closing Day: Wednesday.

Annual Events: Suffolk Agricultural Show at the beginning of June.
Military Tattoo at the end of June.

Places To See

Christchurch Mansion, open all year Tuesday to Saturday 10am to 5pm, Sunday 2.30pm to 4.30pm. Closes at dusk in winter.

Mid-1500s red-brick Tudor country house set in a spacious park. The rooms are beautifully furnished and there are some interesting model ships and doll's houses. The art gallery has original paintings by some famous artists including Constable, Gainsborough and Munnings.

Ipswich Museum & Gallery, High Street. Open all year Tuesday to Saturday 10am to 5pm.

The Museum reveals the town's past, including Saxon weapons and jewellery retrieved from a local cemetery.

Transport Museum, Old Trolleybus Depot, Cobham Road. Phone first for open days on ph (01473) 832 260.

The museum features pedal cycles to trolleybuses, handcarts to fire engines, and is one of the largest collections in Britain.

Pykenham's Gatehouse, Northgate Street, is open May to December on the 1st and 3rd Saturday of the month from 10.30am to 12 noon.

A restored 15th century gatehouse leads to the Archdeacon of Suffolk's headquarters.

Tolly Cobbold Brewery & Brewery Tap, Cliff Road, ph (01473) 281 508, has guided tours all year Saturday & Sunday 11.30am and 2.30pm, and May to September week days at 11.30am.

Built in 1896, the establishment still retains working equipment from the original brewery of 1723. Taste the malt, smell the hops and enjoy a complimentary glass of beer at one of the country's oldest breweries. A must for those interested in beer, heritage and history.

In the Butter Market is a *15th century house* with richly carved plasterwork.

Alton Water, Stutton is one of Suffolk's beautiful lakes, and offers a great day out filled with activities including waterside walks, sailing, windsurfing, bird watching and coarse fishing.

Golf: *Ipswich Golf Club*, Purdis Heath, Bucklesham Road, ph (01473) 728 941. 18 and 9 hole courses set in heathland. Some restrictions apply.

Cruises: MV *Pinmill*. 2 hour cruises on the river Orwell Estuary from Ipswich aboard a 1910 passenger launch. Booking information, ph (01473) 624 047 from June to October.

Boat Hire: *Alton Water Sports Centre*, Holbrook Road, Stutton, ph (01473) 328 408. Hire of wind surfers and sailing dinghies. Summer training courses and day memberships are available. Open April to October.

Bicycle Hire: *Bicycle Doctor*, 18 Bartholomew Street, ph (01473) 259 853. Open daily but advisable to telephone first. Delivery and collection of bicycles, and accessories are available.

Alton Cycle Hire, Alton Water, ph (01473) 328 873. Hire by the hour or day, tandems are also available.

Town Trails: From the information office, St Stephen's Church, there is one mile of signposted walks through historic Ipswich. From May to September, there are also many guided tours.

Tour 2 - Ipswich Country Tour

Leave Ipswich on the A1071 heading towards the town of Lavenham.

Hintlesham

Hintlesham Hall, with its lovely Queen Anne front, was built in the 14th century. The Hall is now a hotel with beautifully appointed rooms and a superb restaurant.

The *Church of St Nicholas*, although in a state of disrepair, has six bells which are still rung.

Continue on the A1071, then turn left.

Hadleigh

Hadleigh is 10 miles west of Ipswich on the B1070, and is a charming mix of ancient and new buildings. The approach into the long village main street is over the River Brett. The embankments have ducks and swans, and in the springtime are ablaze with daffodils. The area was once ruled by a Danish chieftain by the name of Gunthrum, who lived in the village for 12 years. He was buried in a wooden church, which was replaced in the 13th century, and rebuilt again in the 15th century on the original site.

Information Centre: Toppesfield Hall, ph (01473) 823 824.

Hospital: Ipswich and East Suffolk, Heath Road, Ipswich.

Police: High Street.

Market Days: Friday & Saturday.

Early Closing Day: Wednesday.

Places To See

Guildhall, Church Square, is a 15th century timber framed building with two overhanging storeys. The central three storey section was the original Market Hall.

Aldham Common has a memorial to Dr Rowland Taylor a Protestant vicar who refused to hold a Mass and was burnt at the stake in 1555.

Overall House was named after Bishop Overall who helped translate the Authorised Version of the Bible for King James I.

Deanery Tower was built in 1495 and was originally designed to be the entrance to a new rectory.

St Mary's Church is depicted in one of Thomas Gainsborough's landscape paintings.

The Corn Exchange, dated 1813, has marks on the corners of the brickwork on the Eastern side where children would sharpen their slate

TOUR 2

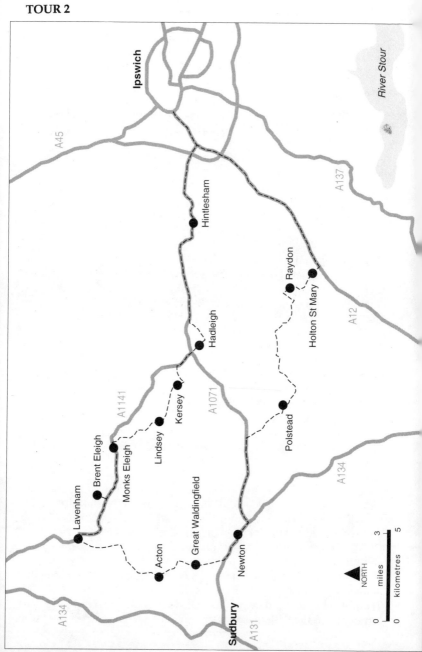

pencils on the way to school. Remains of the medieval kitchen are on the western side of the building.

The *George Inn* has a very nice restaurant and garden, and caters for children. The *Ram Inn* has a restaurant, good bar meals, and children are welcome. The *White Hart Inn* is a beautiful pub, with plenty of atmosphere and charm.

Town Trails: Take a very pleasant 1½ mile stroll along the river Brett, cross the medieval Toppesfield Bridge, turn right and follow the peaceful wooded river path to Bridge Street.

Country Walks: Hadleigh to Raydon is a lovely 2½ mile walk.

Turn right onto the B1170, then turn left.

Kersey

Another one of the *prettiest villages in Suffolk*, on the Lavenham-Hadleigh road. The main street has a ford and rows of dark timbered and painted thatched cottages.

Kersey cloth, a coarse twill weave cloth, was used for making overcoats and army uniforms as the close weave kept out the cold and rain.

St Mary's Church dates from the 14th century and sits on top of the hilltop overlooking this pretty and delightful little village.

The sign of a *horse's tail* hanging from the eaves of a house, was the trade sign of a vet.

The *Bell Inn* in the village centre is a heavily timbered 700-year-old pub, that has been used in films. A lovely place to stop for lunch or dinner, where a blazing fire, exposed beams and warm welcome await. Meals are very good and reasonably priced.

Craft Centres: *Kersey Pottery*, The Street, ph (01473) 822 092. Open Tuesday to Saturday from Easter to Xmas. Weekends only from Xmas. The shop is well stocked with handmade stoneware, etchings and paintings by Suffolk artists.

Turn left, then take the first on the right, along country roads.

Lindsey

St James Chapel is medieval and was once attached to a castle. It is open daily, and well worth a visit.

Heading north, either take the left fork in the road or continue straight ahead, to join the A1141.

Monks Eleigh

A most attractive village with lots of cream coloured painted thatched roof cottages. In the middle of the green stands the village pump. The Hall was rebuilt in 1658.

The *Church of St Peter* dates from the 14th & 15th centuries but the font is even older.

Craft Centres: *Corn Craft*, on the A1141, ph (01449) 740 456. Traditional crafts and corn dollies on display are lovely and the centre is open all year.

Continue on the A1141.

Brent Eleigh

On the road to Sudbury is a little road to the right which leads to Swingleton Green. It's only a one car wide lane and at the end of the road the signpost shows *Swingleton Green only*, its not surprising that the locals want to keep it quiet, it is truly quite unbelievable.

An absolutely fantastic village that is well worth the visit. *Hill Farm Cottage* is beautifully thatched and the accommodation is excellent. The drive around here is definitely a must! *Brent Eleigh Hall* is mainly Elizabethan.

St Mary's Church has a 14th century carved door, wonderful Jacobean woodwork and lovely wall paintings.

Lavenham

Lavenham is probably one of the most photographed towns in England, and has been used in many movies because of its setting in beautiful green countryside. There are many ornate Tudor wooden buildings dating back to the 15th century and some of the houses have a distinct lean to them.

John Constable went to school here, and was friends with Jane Taylor who wrote *Twinkle Twinkle Little Star*.

Lavenham is situated on the A1141, 2 miles east of the A134, between Bury St Edmunds & Sudbury

Information Centre: Lady Street, ph (01787) 248 207. Open from April to September 10am to 4.45pm.

Places To See

The Priory, open April to 31st October 10.30am to 5.30pm.

Beautiful timber-framed Historic House and Garden dating from 1600. The original medieval hall lies in the centre of the building and houses a wonderful Bossanyi Art collection of paintings, drawings and stained glass windows. The Courtyard is paved with York stone from an old threshing mill. The herb garden, enclosed by a yew hedge, contains over 100 species. The refectory restaurant offers delicious home-made cakes and soups, and the filled potatoes in their jackets are wonderful.

Guildhall, Market Place, open April 31 to October daily 11am to 5pm.

The Guildhall of Corpus Christi, built in 1529, is a fine example of a close studded timber building. On one of the corners is a full length figure of Lord de Vere.

Little Hall, open April to October, Wednesday, Thursday, Saturday & Sunday 2.30pm to 6pm.

Outstanding 15th century Hall with a crown post roof. There is a fine collection of Gayer-Anderson antique furniture, paintings and books.

Swan Hotel is one of the oldest and most beautiful English pubs. It dates from the 14th century, has wonderful old exposed beams and a lovely garden, and the accommodation is excellent. The exterior is fantastic and truly English with its white paint, wooden beams and crooked shape.

The *Market Place* is dominated by a 16th century cross.

Angel Corner Hotel has very cosy and relaxed bars with bookshelves, china and paintings on display. The enormous inglenook fireplace is beautiful and very inviting with burning logs in the winter. Sit outside in the spring and summer, and face the Market Place, or relax and enjoy the lovely courtyard at the rear of the hotel.

The *Greyhound* is an olde worlde pub with great atmosphere, serving excellent bar meals and evening meals, all reasonably priced. This is a most delightful pub and should not be missed.

The *Church of St Peter & St Paul* has a 141ft tower, is reputed to be one of the finest in the country, and has richly carved screens. The church bells are also renowned for the tenor bell, made in 1625, that is famous for its perfect tone. Open all year (10am to 3.30pm in winter).

Country Walks: *Lavenham-Long Melford Walk*. 3 mile walk along the disused railway and farm track that links two of Suffolk's most beautiful towns.

> Leave Lavenham, heading south on the B1071, for Sudbury, then take the second turn right.

Acton

This tiny village had a claim to fame when 17-year-old Catherine Foster poisoned her husband in 1846. She was the last woman hanged publicly in Bury St Edmunds. The village pump adjoins three thatched terrace cottages and on the end wall of the last cottage there is a picture of her.

The *Crown* has good bar meals, nice restaurant and an outside garden where children are well catered for with a play area.

> Leave the village heading east, then turn right onto the B1115.

Great Waldingfield

The *Church of St Lawrence* is 14th century, and John Hopkins, a rector in the 16th century, lies buried in the churchyard. He and Thomas Sternhold produced the first version of the Psalms set to music.

> After passing through the village, turn left onto the A134.

Newton Green

The golf course, cottages, beautiful gardens and very large old houses surround the attractive village green. *All Saints' Church* is 14th century and stands in farmland.

The *Saracens Head* is partly Tudor and has a large mounting stone where travellers are thought to have changed horses on their way to east coast ports. The inside is a very cosy, typically English pub with delightful seating around the huge fireplace. The bar meals are excellent and reasonably priced.

> After leaving the village you will come to a junction in the road, take the left road which is the A1071, then take the second on the right.

Polstead

A very pretty little village with neat cottages and tiny gardens overlooking the river Box and Polstead pond. Polstead Hall is a Georgian mansion.

The 12th century *Church of St Mary* is unusual as it has a stone spire and the chancel has brick arches.

Maria Marten was murdered here by her lover in 1827, and a notice board has been erected that tells the tale.

Country Walks: Walk some of the well-marked trails across the common where the views from St Mary's Church to the other side of the valley and Stoke-by-Nayland are magnificent.

> Head east on country roads to the B1070, then turn right.

Raydon

Country Walks: Hadleigh to Raydon is a lovely 2½ mile walk.

> Pass through Holton St Mary on the B1071, then turn left onto the A12 and return to Ipswich.

Tour 3 - Ipswich to Aldeburgh

Leave Ipswich on the A12, turn north-east, then take the first right onto the A1214 and continue into Martlesham.

Martlesham

A large attractive village on the river Deben where St Mary's Church is typically Suffolk, with knapped flint walls, square tower and a churchyard surrounded by tall trees.

The Red Lion is a very popular inn dating back to the 16th century. An attraction is the very brightly painted ship's figurehead supposedly taken from a Dutch ship during the Battle of Sole Bay in 1672.

The Black Tiles Inn, a cafe renowned for home-made cakes and pasties, and where, during the second world war, serviceman based at nearby RAF and USAAF bases used to meet.

Woodbridge

Woodbridge is situated off the A12, 9 miles north-east of Ipswich, and the river Deben bears witness to the town's history of ship-building, rope-making and sail-making. Both Edward III, in the 14th century, and Sir Francis Drake, in the 16th century, used ships built here as fighting ships.

Hospital: Ipswich Hospital, Heath Road, Ipswich.

Police: Grundisburgh Road.

Places To See

Sutton Hoo Archaeological Site is an Anglo Saxon Ship Burial Site and access is by foot from the B1083 at Hollesley. It is open Easter weekend and from May to early September, Saturday & Sunday with guided tours at 2pm and 3pm.

The site is a group of low, grassy mounds overlooking the River Deben. Excavations in 1939 brought to light the richest burial ever discovered in Britain - an Anglo Saxon ship containing a magnificent treasure. It is thought to have been the grave of Raewald, one of the earliest known Kings, who died in 624/625AD. The Sutton Hoo treasure has become one of the principal attractions of the British Museum, but its discovery raised many questions about the site that remain unanswered. Replicas of the treasure are on display in the Woodbridge museum.

Buttrums Mill, Burkitt Road, is open May to September on Saturday & Sunday 2pm to 6pm.

TOUR 3

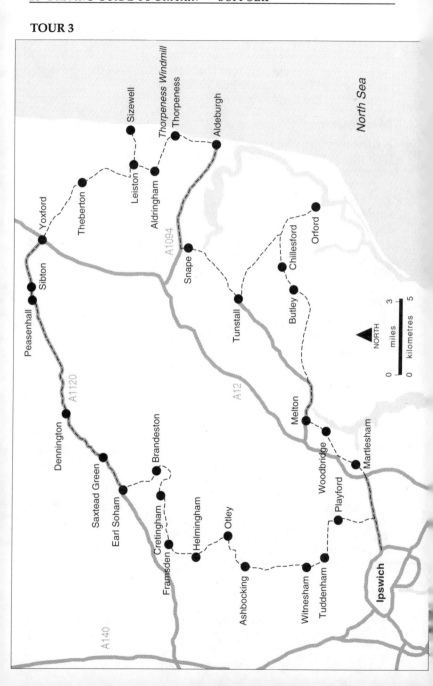

The ground floor of this six-storey brick tower dates from 1836 and contains an historic display of milling machinery and equipment.

Woodbridge Museum on Market Hill is open April to October from Thursday to Saturday 10am to 4pm and Sunday 2.30pm to 4.30pm.

The museum is a history of Woodbridge and its prominent personalities who include Edward Fitzgerald, a poet, Isaac Johnson, surveyor and map maker, Thomas Churchyard, painter, and Thomas Seckford. Fine paintings and artefacts also illustrate the activities of ordinary people in the area.

Tide Mill, Tide Mill Quay, is open May to September daily 11am to 5pm, and in October on Saturday & Sunday 11am to 5pm.

The Mill was built in 1793 and has been restored to full working order.

Shire Hall on Market Hill is a lovely 16th century building.

St Mary's Church has a large 15th century West tower with strange buttresses that seem to change shape as you climb the stairs.

The *Captain's Table*, a lovely restaurant on Quay Street between the town centre and the yacht haven, has a warm and cosy atmosphere, and the personal attention and excellent food make this a popular place.

The *Ye Olde Bell & Steelyard Inn* has a patio and caters for children. Meals are very good and reasonably priced.

The Cherry Tree Inn has excellent food, and meals are served by the fireside in winter in a cosy room decorated with barrels, books and other memorabilia.

Golf: *Woodbridge Golf Course*, Bromeswell Heath, ph (01394) 382 038 has both 9 and 18 hole courses. Handicap certificate is required and restrictions apply to the 18 hole course. Visitors are welcome at weekends and Bank Holidays for the 9 hole course. Both courses are gentle undulating heathland.

Horse Riding: *Popular Park Equestrian Centre*, Heath Road, Hollesley, ph (01394) 411 023. Ride for fun or seriously where the facilities cater for all types of riders with an indoor school, outdoor menages and a show-jumping arena. Novice and Intermediate cross country courses, and wonderful off road hacking over heath and through forests are lovely ways to see the magnificent countryside. Perhaps try the art of carriage driving.

Country Walks: *Fynn Valley Walk* is a wonderful 9 mile walk from Witnesham to Woodbridge.

Leave Woodbridge on the B1084, and turn right at Melton.

Butley

St John the Baptist Church was built in Norman times, but the tower is from the 14th century.

The Mill is still working, although now run by electricity, and has a fine Regency porch. The Mill was mentioned in the Domesday Book and was moved to its present site in 1536.

A *14th century gatehouse* is all that remains of the 11th century Butley Priory, which is now a private residence. The carvings on the gatehouse include national and baronial emblems.

Staverton Thicks has a deer park, and heavily wooded areas of pollard oaks and holly trees. The oldest recorded tree in the park dates from 1540. Take a walk along the footpath around the outside of the park, it's well worth it!.

Butley Clumps, dating from 1790, is an avenue of beech trees originally planted in a *clump of four with a pine tree in the middle of the square*.

The *Oyster Inn* is a nice little pub, partly Elizabethan, that serves very good, reasonably priced meals.

Craft Centres: Butley Pottery & Tea Room, Mill Lane, ph (01394) 450 785. Renovated thatched barn open daily April to September, and from October to March on Wednesday to Sunday, 10.30am to 5pm. The tea room offers lovely home-made cakes and scones and is well worth a visit.

Country Walks: Walk along the footpath around the outside of Staverton Thicks and the deer park.

Continue along the B1084.

Chillesford

A pretty, little village where the *Froize Inn*, an 18th century pub with Tudor sections, is worth a visit.

The *Church of St Peter* was built in the 12th century and stands on a high knoll just outside the village. It has an older tower that is thought to be made of Roman brick.

At the 'T' intersection, turn right.

Orford

A delightful village on the B1084 with great atmosphere and lovely old buildings. The harbour and the approach are wonderful and are well worth a visit for artists, photographers and anglers. The village store carries a great range of goods, and the atmosphere and service is typically village-cheery.

Early Closing Day: Wednesday.

Places To See

Castle Remains are open daily 10am to 6pm Easter to end of October, and 10am to 4pm November to Easter weekend.

The castle retains a 90ft high 18-sided keep built in the 12th century by Henry II. The 10ft deep walls conceal a maze of well preserved rooms and passages. The spiral staircase from the basement to the top of the keep provides magnificent views.

Dunwich Underwater Exploration Exhibition in The Craft Shop, Front Street, is open all year daily 11am to 5pm. Marine archaeology and coastal erosion displays show the exploration of ruins of the former town of Dunwich which is now largely under sea.

The *Kings Head Inn* in the centre of the village is a 13th century smugglers' inn lying on the river Ore. Very popular pub where the accommodation is good and children are welcome in the garden and dining room.

The Jolly Sailor Inn, on Quay Street, is a very popular 16th century pub with an entrance down a step off the street. It has a cosy old fashioned bar with great atmosphere, taking patrons back to the days of the smugglers.

Stop in at the *Old Warehouse* and sample lovely home-made cakes, scones, local fish dishes, vegetarian and traditional meals. Open all year from Tuesday to Sunday including evenings and is licensed. In the summer it is delightful to sit outside and take in the beautiful views of the quay and river.

Cruises: The *Lady Florence*, ph (01831) 698 298, has four hour lunch cruises on the rivers Alde and Ore, passing Aldeburgh, Havergate Island and Shingle Street.

The *Regardless*, ph (01394) 450 637, offers one hour trip round Havergate Island. Departs on the hour daily from 11am except 1pm.

Nature Trails: *Havergate Island*. Reserve with breeding avocets and terns, shingle, saltmarsh and lagoons. Contact the Warden for all the details, including the boat trip.

Tunstall

Very nice old church and rectory. There are many well signposted walks along the forest drive, with plenty of picnic areas and car parking places.

Turn right in Tunstall village onto the B1069.

Snape

Set on the banks of the river Alde, Snape was once able to berth 100-ton sailing barges loaded with malt made from Suffolk barley. The beautiful granaries and malthouses have been converted into one of the largest Concert Halls in the world.

Annual Event: Aldeburgh Festival in June.

Places To See

The *Aldeburgh Festival* is held here annually in June and other concerts are held throughout the year. The Arts & Cultural Centre houses antique, crafts and souvenir shops. Well worth a visit.

The *Captain's Cabin* in the High Street, is a warm and cosy pub with great atmosphere, inexpensive meals and very generous servings, especially if you are after good home-made soup and pies.

The *Crown Inn* overlooks the marshes, and it was from one of its dormer windows that the 'all clear' sign would be given to smugglers, allowing them to bring their illegal goods up the river.

The *Plough & Sail* is a traditional country pub with a well-stocked bar that offers good meals using local produce and fresh fish.

The *Golden Key* is a very comfortable 16th century beamed pub, where game is on the menu along with the traditional roasts and fish and chips. Children are welcome to the lovely garden area.

Country Walks: Take a leisurely 3 mile walk along the tow path to Iken Church.

Cruises: Well worth taking the one hour boat trip on the river Alde aboard the *Edward Alan John*, a covered boat that takes up to 70 passengers. Departure times are dependent on the tides.

Leave Snape on the A1094, and head east for the coast.

Aldeburgh

Aldeburgh, on the A1094, was a prosperous port with a flourishing shipbuilding industry in the 16th century. The shipyards built the famous *Greyhound* and *Pelican* for Drake, and the men of Aldeburgh sailed them. The River Alde is now a haven for yachtsmen.

The beach is pebbled and it is possible to walk to Thorpeness and the windmill, past North Warren Reserve. This is one of the oldest seaside resorts, and has lots of guest houses, cottages and old buildings. The shoulder of the harbour has been reclaimed, and the fishermen draw up their boats on to the beach and sell their fish. This town with its wide street is a fascinating town, and well worth a stroll around the interesting shops.

Information Centre: The Cinema, High Street, ph (01728) 453 637 - open summer only.

Hospital: Aldeburgh Cottage Hospital, Park Road.

Police: Leiston Road.

Places To See

Moot Hall is open April & May, Saturday & Sunday 2.30pm to 5pm; June & September daily 2.30pm to 5pm; July & August daily 10am to

12.30pm & 2.30pm to 5pm.

This is a 16th century timber-framed building with end walls of brick that was once used as an open market. The tall chimneys are 16th century, but most of the building was restored in 1855. Moot Hall was once in the centre of town, and it now houses exhibits of town history and maritime affairs including prints and relics of the Snape Anglo-Saxon ship burial site.

Martello Tower, on the seafront, is a tall square building with a spiral staircase on the outside and is one of many built along the East Anglian coast in the period 1810 to 1812 as defences against Napoleon. *Alde House*, was the home of Elizabeth Anderson who entered the medical profession when it was still closed to women. She opened a hospital in London which still bears her name, and was also the first woman mayor in England, when she became mayor of Aldeburgh.

The *Church of St Peter and St Paul* is mostly 16th century, although the tower is about 200 years older, and it stands on a hill overlooking town and sea. There are several interesting Elizabethan brasses and an elaborate pulpit dated 1632.

Ye Old Cross Keys Inn, on the seafront near the lifeboat, is a typical 16th century fisherman's haunt, and is still very popular. Local seafood could never be fresher, as it comes straight to the kitchen from the boats. The outside garden bar, where children are also welcome, has great views to the sea.

For some of the best fish and chips, pay a visit to the *Fish & Chip Shop* in the High Street.

Wine: Visit the small vineyard on Leiston Road, ph (01728) 452 135 for an appointment. Set in large gardens, the vineyard is the most easterly in the country and visitors can sample some of the great local wine.

Golf: *Aldeburgh Golf Club*, ph (01728) 452 890. 18 and 19 holes on heathland courses where restrictions apply at weekends.

Head up the coast road to Thorpeness.

Thorpeness

Thorpeness Windmill is open May, June & September on Saturday & Sunday 2pm to 5pm; July & August daily 2pm to 5pm. It is a mock Tudor water tower disguised as a house, and is known as *The House in the Clouds*.

Gallery Coffee Shop, Barn Hall, is a licensed restaurant next to the beach with a pleasant garden overlooking the boating lake. Enjoy a cream tea or choose from the selection of rich gateaux. Local crafts are displayed and are for sale.

Golf: *Thorpeness Golf Club & Hotel*, ph (01728) 452 176. 18 holes, undulating heathland course with a water hazard. Restrictions apply at the weekends.

Boat Hire: Hire a rowing boat or canoe and see Thorpeness Mere. Open Easter to October daily.

> Leave the town on the B1353.

Aldringham

Nature Reserve: Heathland, reedbed and coastal grazing marshes. Access is from the car park off the Aldeburgh/Leiston road or by footpath off the Aldeburgh/Thorpeness road.

Craft Centre: *Craft Market*, ph (01728) 830 397. Open Monday to Saturday 10.15am to 5.30pm and Sunday 12noon to 2pm. The market has three galleries providing friendly surroundings. High quality ceramics, paintings, jewellery, gifts and many other crafts are on display and are for sale. There is a children's play area, and a coffee shop offers light refreshments.

> Head north onto the B1122.

Leiston

Police: 34 King's Road.

Long Shop Museum, Main Street is open April to October, daily 10am to 5pm and Sunday 11am to 5pm. It was restored in 1853, and has one of the earliest examples of steam engines.

The Abbey remains are open daily, except in winter. The Abbey was founded on the Minsmere marshes in 1182, and moved from its original site in 1363. An octagonal brick gate-turret is all that remains.

White Horse Hotel in Station Road is an 18th century hotel with a homely interior, excellent food, and a wonderfully well-stocked bar. The garden area is well equipped for children.

> Take the coast road in the centre of town if you wish to visit the power station.

Sizewell

The Visitor Centre is open all year daily 10am to 4pm, except on Sunday from October to March. Guided tours of power stations are available by arrangement, ph (01728) 642 139.

An exhibition of nuclear energy, power and the environment is housed in the Visitor Centre.

> Leave Leiston on the B1122 and pass through the pretty village of Theberton, with its small church. Cross the A12.

Yoxford

An attractive village in the *Garden of Suffolk*. Stoneware pots, local preserves, cured ham, home-made bread and cakes make this village worth a stop.

> Pass through Sibton and Peasenhall on the A1120.

Dennington

Very pretty little village where the post office is recorded as being one of the oldest in the country and has been in the same building since 1830.

The *Queens Head*, built in the late 1600s, is a lovely pub with great atmosphere.

The *Church of St Mary* was built in the 14th century and is the resting place of Lord Bardolph, who was buried here in the 15th century.

The 15th century screens, complete with lofts and parapets, and the 14th century carved chancel windows and carved pews are some of the best in Suffolk.

Saxtead Green

A pretty little village with a large *green* opposite the main attraction, the mill.

Saxtead Post Mill, ph (01728) 685 789, is open April to September from Monday to Saturday 10am to 1pm and 2pm to 6pm. It is an elegant 18th century white post mill with roundhouse. The base of the mill contains mill stones, and the machinery in the body revolves on a central post.

Manor Farm is moated and dates from the mid-15th century.

Earl Soham

The long village street has a row of 16th and 17th century steep thatched cottages in a setting of beech, poplar and elm trees. This very attractive village has been a winner of the *Best Kept Village* award. Visit the village shop and meet the butcher who still wears a striped apron and boater hat, and the grocer who delivers the villagers' goods by bicycle.

Earl Soham Lodge is a moated manor house.

The half timber-framed 15th century pub *Falcon Inn* is very characteristic of this village. The log fire, cosy bars, ancient timbers and good meals, along with the warmth and friendliness, make this a very welcome stop. Children are catered for and are welcome in the restaurant. Accommodation is good and the views from the windows are excellent, looking across the magnificent countryside.

St Mary's Church dates from the 13th century, but has a 15th century tower. The buttresses bear an inscription to some of its builders.

Leave the village, and take the first road left through beautiful countryside.

Brandeston

Very pretty countryside with dairy farms on the roadside, where you expect to see cows still being milked by hand. The approach into this lovely village with its row of beautiful thatched cottages, village shop and post office is well worth a visit. *Brandeston Hall*, built in 1543, is now a preparatory school for Framlingham College.

The *Queens Head*, built in 1813, is very nice and offers good, reasonably-priced bar meals.

All Saints' Church has a 13th century font although the church is supposedly much older. There is a grave in the churchyard of Nicholas Revett, a landscaper, who died in 1804. Among his landscape commissions was West Wycombe Park in Buckinghamshire.

Turn right in the village.

Cretingham

Cretingham has a village sign that is very unusual as it has two different panels. One side shows a typical Anglo-Saxon farming scene, and the other side shows a family sailing up the river Deben.

The *Cretingham Bell*, a 16th century tudor building that was once a manor house, has been beautifully renovated and retains flagged floors, beams and open dining areas. Families are well catered for with a well-equipped garden and family room. Barbecues are held on Sunday throughout the summer.

The original *Bell Inn* was used in 1887 as a court room to decide the fate of Rev Gilbert-Cooper, the curate who supposedly murdered the vicar Rev William Farley. The curate was found guilty and sent to Broadmoor prison, where he subsequently died.

Golf: *Cretingham Golf Course*. 9 holes in the lovely Deben Valley. Restrictions apply, worth phoning first.

Framsden

Framsden Windmill is open weekends all year by appointment only, ph (01473) 890 328. It is a tall post mill dating from 1760 and is still working.
    Just the most beautiful countryside through here, real post card scenery.

> Turn left onto the B1077.

Helmingham

Helmingham Hall Gardens, ph (01473) 890 363, are open Sunday 2pm to 6pm from early May to September.
    A magnificent moat and walled gardens surround a beautiful Tudor Hall. The gardens boast some very fine Herbaceous and Spring borders, as well as a wild flower garden and a large collection of roses. The old *Coach House* offers home-made cakes, and the scones with cream are most enjoyable. In the park take a Safari ride and see the herds of red and fallow deer, Highland cattle and Soay sheep. The House is not open to the public.

> In the village, turn left onto a country road, which is well signposted for Otley.

Otley

Otley Hall, ph (01473) 890 264 for open days, is a 15th century moated medieval hall. Rich in architecture and family history, it is set in 10 acres of garden, that include a canal, mount, nuttery, rose and herbaceous gardens.
Thirteenth century *St Mary's Church* has a unique and very interesting baptistery font which is 6ft long and 2ft 8ins deep. The font is always full as the water level maintains itself naturally.

> At the 'T' intersection in the village turn left, and at the next 'T' intersection turn right. At the crossroads with the B1077 turn right.

Ashbocking

Wine: *James White Apple Juice & Cider Co*, White Fruit Farm. Open all year Monday to Friday 10am to 4pm, ph (01473) 890 111. Cider and apple juice tasting. Cider pressing can be seen October to February.

Witnesham

Little hamlet with the *Barley Mow Inn* and a couple of little cottages.
Country Walks: *Fynn Valley Walk* is a lovely 9 mile walk from Witnesham to Woodbridge.

> Continue on the B1077 then turn left for Tuddenham St Martin.

Tuddenham St Martin

The *Church of St Martin* stands high on the hill overlooking this very pretty little village. The church is Norman, the font dates from 1443, and the pews are mostly 15th century.

> Follow country lanes left then right to Playford.

Playford

A very small and pretty village with a post office/store and a cluster of houses around the green.

The *Church of St Mary* stands high on the hill. Go through the lychgate, up the steep ascent to the magnificent doorway of one of only two churches in Britain to have an upright brass. The brass is that of Sir George Felbrigge once owner of Playford and large estates in Norfolk.

The two pre-Reformation bells in the tower are still rung every Sunday, as they have been for over 500 years.

> Head south to the A1214 and return to Ipswich.

Tour 4 - Ipswich to Easton and Framlingham

Leave Ipswich on the A1214 (east). At the A12, turn left, then take the 3rd left turn to Great Bealings. The roads are all well signposted.

Great Bealings

Very old and pretty village with a store and post office, where *St Mary's Church* stands in a meadow. Walk up the path to the porch dedicated to the memory of Sir Thomas Seckford founder of Woodbridge School and almshouses.

Bealings House was built in 1770 and stands in beautiful parkland.

Take the left fork from Great Bealings, then turn right.

Grundisburgh

Beautiful little village pronounced *Grunsburo* on the river Lark. The 14th century *Church of St Mary* is built on older foundations. The village store, *The Old Forge*, supplies almost everything and the *Dog Inn* is the only remaining pub in the village.

Turn left onto the B1079.

Clopton

This little village on the B1079 has two churches, a beautiful old Manor house set amongst trees, and a lovely thatched farm and cottages, making this a very pleasant drive along really narrow laneways.

Turn right onto the B1078 where the surrounding countryside is wonderful. Take the fourth turn left, a very short narrow lane, then turn to the left to Easton, over a little hump back bridge and past Clevering Mill Golf Course.

Clevering Hall is beautiful but not open to the public.

Continue along country roads, through scenic countryside.

TOUR 4

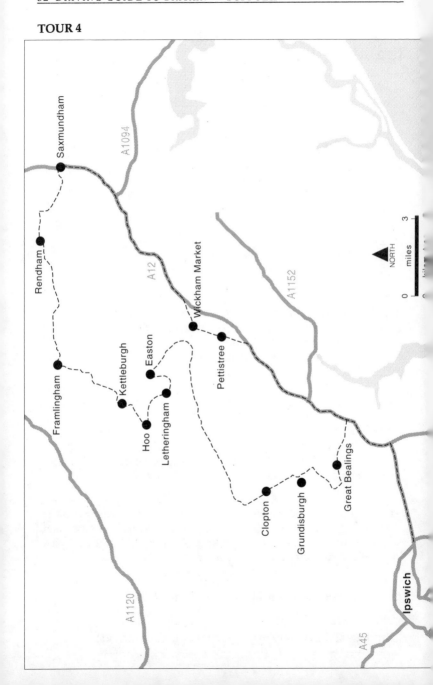

Easton

The approach is lovely into Easton, very nice scenic drive past farms where cows are milked in farmyards on the roadside. The countryside around here is fantastic and well worth a visit. The *White Horse Inn* is a lovely pub offering a friendly and homely atmosphere in a most delightfully picturesque village.

Easton Farm Park is a working farm that is open daily from 10.30am to 6pm, mid-March to early October. Visitors can feed the animals, watch the blacksmith at work, or visit the dairy where cows are milked in this Victorian Country Farm Park.

Leave Easton on the road to Hoo, then turn left.

Letheringham

Water Mill & Gardens, ph (01728) 746 349, are open end March to end May, and early July to end August.

A newly restored wheel has been added to this 18th century working mill set in 5 acres of beautiful gardens with river walks and meadows. The aviary with its exotic pheasants is worth visiting.

Pass through Hoo staying on the same road, then turn left.

Kettleburgh

Very pretty with picturesque farms leading into the village where there is a delightful little pub called *The Checkers* which has tiny square glass windows.

St Andrew's Church has a 14th century tower and was once in the village centre. It now stands on high ground overlooking the village.

Framlingham

Framlingham is an old market town dominated by the Castle, and on market day you can just about buy everything.

Of particular interest are its two Victorian post boxes.

Visit the *Crown Inn* in the middle of the market square where you can relax in lovely cosy surroundings and enjoy a hearty bar meal.

Market Day: Saturday.

Early Closing Day: Wednesday.

Annual Events: Spring Bank Holiday Monday Fair.

The Castle has special events.

Places To See

The Castle and *Lanham Museum* are open daily Easter to September from 10.30am to 1pm & 2pm to 4.30pm, November to March 10am to 4pm.

The Castle's existing walls and square towers are thought to have been built in the early 1200s. Around the massive walls are 13 towers with a walkway linking nine of them. Inside the walls, the castle's history and varied uses over the centuries are reflected in a fascinating mixture of historical styles. It was here that Queen Mary I's supporters rallied to her in 1553 after the attempt to set Lady Jane Grey on the throne, while in Elizabeth I's reign Framlingham was used as a prison for rebellious priests.

Lanham Museum, within the castle grounds, has exhibits of domestic bygones, and farm and craft tools.

The *Meres* is a bird sanctuary managed by the Suffolk Wildlife Trust. The castle overlooks the meres and there is a circular walk. In winter when the lake is iced over, skaters come from miles around and it's a very pretty sight to watch them skate with the aid of car headlights.

Framlingham College is a Gothic Revival style building on the Dennington Road.

The *Church of St Michael* is Perpendicular, and has an outstanding hammerbeam roof and a magnificent organ case dated 1674.

Wine: *Shawsgate Vineyard*, Badingham Road, ph (01728) 724 060. 17 acre vineyard with its own winery. Open Easter to end of October between 10.30am to 5pm. Admission charge includes vineyard walk, winery tour, wine tasting and film. The vineyard has its own restaurant, play area and shop.

Onto the B1119 for Saxmundham, pass through Rendham. Turn right onto the A12, then turn right for Wickham Market.

Wickham Market

This is a straggling village on the upper reaches of the river Deben. The 14th century *All Saint's Church* has an octagonal tower surmounted by a tall leaded spire rising about 140ft.

Valley Farm Camargue Horses is open all year Thursday to Tuesday from 10am to 4pm. This is Britain's only breeding herd of these horses from the South of France.

At Boulge, 2½ miles south-west, Edward FitzGerald the translator of *The Rubiat of Omar Khayyam* is buried. On his grave is a rose bush from Omar Khayyam's grave in Iran.

Leave Wickham Market heading south, not on the A12, but along a country road.

Pettistree

Delightful little country village with pretty thatched cottages and houses. The *Greyhound Inn* is a heavily beamed, very warm and welcoming pub with log fires in the winter.

The *Church of St Peter and St Paul* is 15th century with more recent additions. The pews are richly carved and there are 16th century brasses of Francis Bacon and his two wives. One local story relates how tramps used to bury their money in the graveyard and then dig it up when they were leaving the village. Rogues Lane is supposedly where money was usually buried.

Leave the village heading east for the A12, then turn right. Return to Ipswich.

TOUR 5

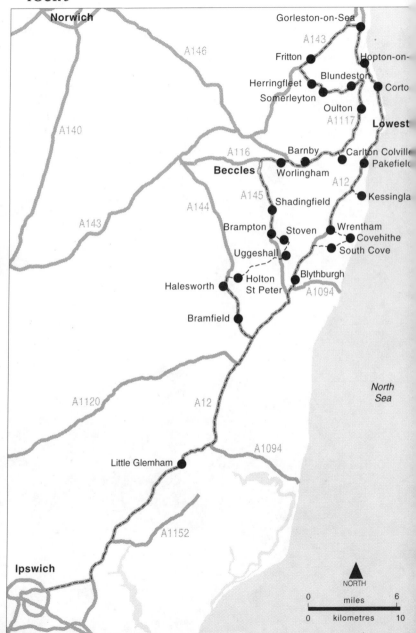

Tour 5 - Ipswich to Lowestoft

Leave Ipswich on the A12.

Little Glemham

The *Bell Inn* is a beautiful Suffolk pink, thatched roof pub. The open fireplace and cosy bar make this a definite stop, where the welcome is warm and friendly. A good selection of reasonably priced meals are served with generous portions. The garden setting is lovely and children are well catered for with a play area and pets' corner.

The *Lion Inn*, has exposed timber beams, some of which are believed to have been taken from a 16th century ship, and a lovely brick fireplace and cosy bar. The garden has an aviary and children are welcome.

Blythburgh

Small village on the River Blyth is set in very pretty countryside. On the approach into the village the magnificent spires and towers of the church dominate the landscape.

The *Church of the Holy Trinity* was built in the 15th century and is 127ft long and 54ft wide. The pillars still bear the scars of the time when Cromwell used the nave as a stable. There is a wealth of medieval treasures within the church. Open 8am to 4pm in winter and 8am to 7.30pm in summer.

Nature Reserves: *Norman Gwatkin Reserve* is a large area of marsh and fen with alder and willow coppice, walkway and 2 hides.

Craft Centres: *Blythburgh Pottery, Dorothy Midson Ceramics,* behind the Post Office, Chapel Road. Suffolk's smallest working pottery. Open all year 11am to 5pm.　•

After passing the Wangford turn-off, take the third road on the right (before Frostenden) and pass through South Cove.

Covehithe

The *Church of St Andrew* was built in the 14th and 15th century, and has been a great inspiration to artists. It is set within the ruins of a larger church and is worth seeing as it is quite eerie. It is open during daylight hours.

The road continues past the church, so only pedestrians can access the cliff top and beautiful sandy beach.

> Take the right fork in the road.

Wrentham

Very pretty little village. The *Five Bells* is a lovely pub on the Covehithe Road.

It is a beautiful drive along the tree-lined narrow lane leading to the 15th century church of St Nicholas.

Bicycle Hire: *Cedar Cycles*, Tower Mills, Southwold Road. Open all year.

Craft Centres: *Wrentham Basketware*, London Road. English willow basket making workshop with over 320 traditional styles from flower baskets to hampers.

> On the A12 turn right, then turn right onto the B1437.

Kessingland

The Domesday Book records that in the reign of William the Conqueror, the village had to pay the Lord of the Manor 22,000 herrings.

The *Church of St Edmund* with its 96ft tower is a village landmark.

Suffolk Wildlife Park is open daily from 10am to 6.30pm. The wildlife park stands in 100 acres of woodland. There are three Explorer walking trails, or visitors can take a train ride and see the Safari Park in style. Lions, Cheetahs, Camels, Zebras, Chimpanzees, Parrots and Monkeys can all be seen from the lake-side walk. Stroll along the Flamingo walk and see these beautiful birds at home by the pool. There is also a farmyard corner where children can feed the animals.

> Turn right back onto the A12 and pass through Pakefield where two churches share the same building and churchyard.

Lowestoft

The town of Lowestoft is on the A12. Fishing has been its main industry since the middle of the last century, and there are guided tours of the harbour and fish market, and often a trawler is available for viewing. The outer harbour is the home of the yacht club and Lowestoft lifeboat station, founded in 1801.

The old town, behind the harbour, is criss-crossed by attractive old cobbled lanes known as The Scores.

Lowestoft was the birthplace of Thomas Nash, poet and dramatist, and of composer Benjamin Britten.

Information Centre: East Point Pavilion, Royal Plain, ph (01502) 523 000.

Hospital: Lowestoft & North Suffolk Hospital, Tennyson Road.

Police: Old Nelson Street.

Market Days: Friday, Saturday & Sunday.

Early Closing Day: Thursday.

Places To See

Lowestoft & East Suffolk Maritime Museum, Whapload Road, is open May to September daily from 10am to 5pm.

The Maritime Museum houses fishing and commercial boat models, drifter's cabin, fishing gear, paintings and other memorabilia.

Royal Naval Patrol Service Museum, Sparrow's Nest, is open mid-May to mid-October from Monday to Friday 10am to 12noon and 2pm to 4.30pm; Sunday 2pm to 4.30pm.

The Museum has some fine ship's models, naval documents, uniforms and paintings.

Boatworld, Harbour Road, Oulton Broad, ph (01502) 574 441, is open Monday to Friday from 10am to 4pm. See traditional boat building skills and visit the well-stocked Maritime bookshop.

Fishing Industry Tour from mid July to September. For booking information ph (01502) 523000. Fish market tours leave the information centre at 10am most weekdays.

Oulton Broad is about one mile from the entrance into Lowestoft, and has been awarded *English Beach of the Year*. Very pretty and worth a visit to the wide, sandy beaches and inland lakes.

The *Church of St Margaret* is a memorial to the seafarers and is open from June to September 10am to 4pm.

Golf: *Rookery Park Golf Club*, Beccles Road, Carlton Colville, ph (01502) 560 380. 18 holes plus 9 hole par 3, flat parkland course. Restrictions apply.

Country Walks & Nature Trails: *Beccles Marsh Trail* - circular walks starting from the Quay.

Foxburrow Wood is delightful in Spring with flowers.

Leathes Ham is open water with reeds and woodland.

Cruises: *Waveney River Tours*, Mutford Lock, Bridge Road, ph (01502) 574 903. Broads river trips and day boat hire.

Lowestoft Harbour Boat Tours, ph (01502) 730 514. See Lowestoft from the water. Boat angling trips October to May.

Take the coast road and pass through Corton and Hopton-on-Sea, drive back onto the A12, then turn right.

Gorleston-on-Sea

Ideal spot to use as a base for exploring the many beauty spots in East Anglia on the River Yare, and only three miles south of Great Yarmouth. Lovely safe, sandy beaches and wind surfing, sailing and walking are some of the activities offered in this very attractive seaside town. Accommodation, from hotels to guest houses and self-contained flats, is plentiful and within easy reach of the beach.

Hospital: James Paget Hospital, Lowestoft Road.

The *Church of St Andrew* has two aisles which both run the length of the church and there is an interesting brass (memorial) of a knight dating from 1320.

Golf: *Gorleston Golf Club*, Warren Road, ph (01493) 662 103. 18 holes, cliff side course.

Cross the A12 then take the A143. Pass through Fritton and turn left after Fritton Lake.

Herringfleet

St Olaves Priory is open any reasonable time and the key is available at the Priory House. All that remains is the 14th century undercroft which has a brick vaulted ceiling.

Herringfleet Drainage Windmill is a 19th century smock-mill in working order. Access is by foot only, and it is open on occasional Sundays, ph (01473) 265 162.

Follow the B1074 through Somerleyton.

Somerleyton

The village is situated 5 miles north-west of Lowestoft.

Early Closing Day: Tuesday.

Somerleyton Hall & Gardens, ph (01502) 730 224, is open April, May, June & September on Sunday and Thursday. July & August open Tuesday, Wednesday, Thursday and Sunday 2pm to 5pm. Gardens open from 12.30pm.

The Elizabethan Hall of red brick was re-built in 1846 and contains fine paintings, woodcarvings and stately rooms. 12 acres of gardens are set among beautiful trees and shrubs, while the Victorian greenhouses provide many attractive flowers. The highlight of the garden is the clipped yew maze which is spectacular.

The Loggia Tea Rooms, set in the grounds of the Hall, provide very good cream teas and fresh home-made cooking in spacious and very friendly surroundings.

A miniature railway runs on Sunday and Thursday from 3pm, and is well worth the visit.

Leave the village and head east along a scenic country road.

Blundeston

The Norman *Church of St Mary* has an 11th century south door, and the tallest, thinnest round tower in East Anglia.

Blundeston House was designed by Sir John Soames in 1785, and now houses a prison within the grounds.

In Charles Dicken's classic *David Copperfield* the main character was born at Blundeston and spent holidays here with the Peggotty family.

The *Plough Inn* dates from 1701 and has become famous because of *David Copperfield*. Oak panelling, exposed beams with high back settles, and open fires in the winter, make this pub worth a stop. Bar meals are excellent and reasonably priced. The home-made soups are wonderful as are the hot potatoes filled with a variety of delicious fillings.

Back onto the A12 turn right.

Oulton

Annual Events: Oulton Broad Regatta Week in August.

Lowestoft Museum, Broad House, Everitt Park, ph (01502) 511 457, is open April to mid-May on Saturday & Sunday from 2 to 5pm; mid-May to early October from Monday to Saturday 10.30am to 1pm & 2pm to 5pm and Sunday 2pm to 5pm; October only Saturday & Sunday 2pm to 4pm.

The Museum houses exhibits of local history and a fine collection of Lowestoft china, fossils, flints and other medieval artefacts.

Boatworld, Harbour Road, Oulton Broad, ph (01502) 574 441, is open Monday to Friday 10am to 4pm. Watch traditional boat building skills and visit the well-stocked Maritime bookshop.

Oulton Broad is one of the finest stretches of inland water in the country and offers boats for hire, coarse fishing, sailing regattas and motor-boat races.

The *Church of St Mark* was built in 1884.

By-pass Lowestoft, take the A146.

Carlton Colville

East Anglia Transport Museum is open May to September Sunday 11am to 5pm; June to end September on Saturday 2 to 4pm. Free car park entrance via Hedley House Hotel on the B1384.

The museum has a collection of trolleybuses from five countries. Take a ride on the tram through woodland or take a trip on the 2ft gauge railway.
The *Church of St Peter* dates back to 1473. It was restored in the 19th century when the remains of two earlier buildings were incorporated.
The village has three pubs, the *Crown* on Beccles Road, the *Bell Inn* and the *Old Red House* in The Street.
Golf: *Rookery Park Golf Club*, Beccles Road, ph (01502) 560 380. 18 holes plus 9 holes, flat parkland course. Restrictions apply.
Nature Reserves: *Carlton Marshes*. Access is by the Waveney Way footpath. The reserve is a grazing marsh and fen.

Continue along the A146.

Barnby

The *Church of St John the Baptist* dates from 1200 and contains many interesting items such as a 1410 wall tapestry and the bell in the tower which has an inscription: *may the bell of St John resound for many years*.

The village boasts a shop, garden nursery, riding school and snail farm.

Continue along the A146, then take the third turn on the left.

Worlingham

Very little is left of this old village. *Worlingham Hall* is the present home of Lord Colville of Culross.

All Saints' Church is 13th century and was the church for Worlingham Magna. Worlingham Parva had the *Church of St Mary the Virgin and St Peter*. The two parishes merged in the 15th century.
In 1980, when the old thatched school was being demolished to make way for the new road, skeletons were unearthed and were later re-interred in the churchyard with a headstone to mark the grave.

Beccles

Most of the old town was destroyed by fires in the 16th and 17th centuries. Georgian houses of red-brick make this a very lovely and distinctive town on the River Waveney. West of the Old Market is *St*

Peter's House which is Georgian and has an original Gothic fireplace.

Information Centre: The Quay, Fen Lane, ph (01502) 713 196 - open summer only.

Hospital: Beccles & District War Memorial Hospital, St Mary's Road.

Police: London Road.

Market Day: Friday.

Early Closing Day: Wednesday.

Annual Event: Regatta in July and August.

Places To See

Roos Hall is mostly gabled and dates from 1583. It was once the home of Sir John Suckling, an ancestor of Lord Nelson.

Beccles & District Museum, Newgate, is open April to October on Wednesday, Saturday & Sunday 2.30pm to 5pm; November to March on Sunday only 2.30pm to 5pm.

Local history exhibits include a 19th century printing press, farm implements, costumes and an original town sign.

William Clowes Printing Museum, ph (01502) 712 884, has guided factory tours June to August on Monday to Friday 2pm to 4pm.

The Museum shows the development of printing from 1800 with machinery, woodcuts, books, etc.

The 14th century *St Michael's Church* has a 97ft stone faced tower with 10 bells that stands apart from the church.

Golf: *Wood Valley Golf Club*, The Common, ph (01503) 712 244. 9 holes and restrictions apply.

Take the A145 south.

Shadingfield

The *Church of St John the Baptist* has stood between the two hills for more than 800 years.

The *Fox Inn*, a 16th century coaching inn is a collector's dream with bottles, horse memorabilia, irons and tools adorning the walls. The bars have natural red brick walls and the chairs are certainly different. Meals are excellent, home-made and very reasonably priced.

> Continue south along the A145.

Brampton

Small village with a lovely pub called *The Dog Inn*, and a village pond complete with ducks.

> Turn left.

Stoven

Very pretty little village of a few cottages and a pub.

> Turn right, and then right again.

Uggeshall

The Church is a thatched stone, flint and wood building and is quite unbelievable and really worth a visit.

> Cross the A145 then take the first turn left.

Holton St Peter

Holton St Peter Mill is open Spring & August Bank Holidays and other times by appointment, ph (01986) 872 367. The exterior can be viewed at all reasonable times.

The post mill, built in 1752, sits among pine woods overlooking the very attractive little village.

Church of St Peter has a round Norman tower, a 15th century octagonal font, and a 16th century pulpit.

Halesworth

Hospital: Patrick Stead Hospital, Bungay Road.
Police: Norwich Road.
Places To See
Halesworth & District Museum, Steeple End, is open May to September on Wednesday & Saturday from 10.30am to 12.30 and Wednesday & Sunday 2 to 4.30pm.

The Museum has local displays of geology and archaeology, including fossils, pre-historic flints and medieval finds from recent excavations.

Art Gallery, Steeple End, is open mid-May to mid-September on

Monday to Saturday 11am to 5pm and Sunday 2pm to 5pm.

The Elizabethan House gallery has fine paintings and sculptures. The *White Hart*, in the town centre, is a 17th century pub with lots of charm, inglenook fireplaces, old beams and cottage furniture. Meals are excellent and traditional home cooking is the order of the day.

Golf: St Helena Golf Club, Bramfield Road, ph (01986) 875 567. 18 hole and 9 hole courses and has a floodlit driving range.

Continue south on the A144.

Bramfield

Beautiful thatched church with a round tower set in a very pretty little village. Bramfield House is now a residential Boys Home.

Drive back onto the A12, then turn right for Ipswich.

TOUR 6

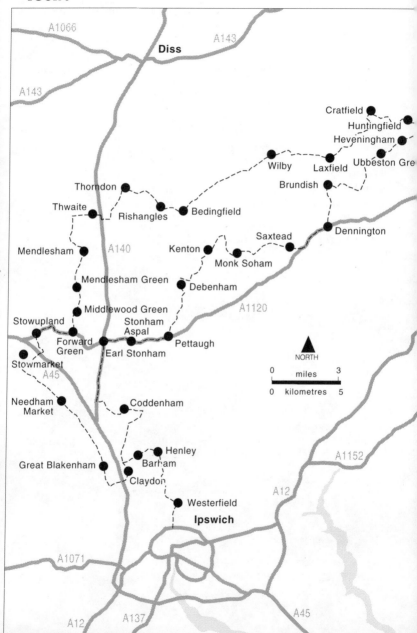

A1066

Diss

A143

A143

Cratfield
Huntingfield
Heveningham
Wilby
Laxfield
Ubbeston Gre
Brundish
Thorndon
Thwaite
Rishangles
Bedingfield
Dennington
Mendlesham
A140
Kenton
Saxtead
Monk Soham
Mendlesham Green
Debenham
Middlewood Green
A1120
Stowupland
Stonham
Aspal
Forward
Green
Pettaugh
Earl Stonham
Stowmarket
A45

NORTH

0   miles   3
0   kilometres   5

Needham
Market
Coddenham
Henley
Great Blakenham
Barham
Claydon
A1152
Westerfield
Ipswich
A12
A1071
A12   A137   A45

Tour 6 - Ipswich Country Village Tour

> Leave Ipswich on the A45, heading for Stowmarket, turn left and pass through Great Blakenham on the B1113.

Needham Market

A small town in the Gipping Valley, Needham Market has some very attractive buildings.

Annual Event: Spring Bank Holiday Monday Fair.

Early Closing Day: Tuesday.

Country Walks: 17 mile long footpath following the river, formerly the Gipping Navigation tow-path, runs between Ipswich and Stowmarket. Circular walks of between 4 and 7 miles are based on the river path and extend into surrounding countryside.

Craft Centres: *The Old Piggery Pottery*, Alder Carr Farm, off Hawks Mill Street, ph (01449) 677 616 after 6pm. Open workshop with handmade earthenware pottery. Open February to December from Tuesday to Sunday 9am to 5pm. There is also a farm shop.

> Continue along the B1113. Cross the A45 onto the A1120.

Stowupland

Quaint little village with a store and a couple of lovely thatched cottages that make this a real treat to visit.

The *Crown* is a beautiful thatched pub, well worth stopping for a meal or a pint in lovely cosy surroundings.

The *Retreat* has a restaurant, good bar meals reasonably priced and a garden where children are well catered for.

> Turn right.

Forward Green

Drive past the green and the *Shepherd and Dog*, a very popular pub near the cricket pitch that serves good reasonably priced bar meals and has a garden that caters for children.

> Turn left and pass through Middlewood Green and Mendlesham Green.

Mendlesham

St Mary's Church contains a unique collection of parish armour which has been here since 1593.

The *Fleece* in Front Street has an original pump that was for villagers who had no access to a private well.

> Turn right and head north along sometimes narrow, scenic country roads. All roads are well signposted.

Thwaite

A very pretty little village where St George's Church has a wooden gargoyle.

The *Bucks Head* is a very nice 15th century pub where the landlord offers a very warm welcome to all in the beamed bar covered with horse brasses. The cosy little restaurant offers good meals which are reasonably priced. Children are well catered for with their own menu and also have a playground in the lovely garden.

> Turn right onto the A140. Take the first turn left and at the 'T' intersection turn left again. Pass through Thorndon and Rishangles. Take the left fork in the road just past the village, then take the second on the left .

Bedingfield

Fleming's Hall is dated 1309 and has to be one of the most beautiful and gracious houses in Suffolk. The moat was added in the late 1500s.

> Turn left.

Wilby

St Mary's Church is 15th century and has beautifully carved pews, two old wall paintings, and a tower that boasts one of the best sounding rings of eight bells in the country.

Craft Centres: on the B1118, ph (01379) 384 253. A lovely row of thatched roof cottages which have been converted into a tea shop and pottery shop. Very good quality home-made pottery in Terracotta or Stoneware is made here. Enjoy a real treat of home-made cakes, pastries, and savoury dishes.

Cross the B1116.

Laxfield

Laxfield & District Museum, Guildhall, High Street, ph (01986) 798 393, is open late May to end September and it is best to phone ahead to confirm times.

The Museum has geology and natural history exhibits, farm and domestic tools, a Victorian kitchen, village shop displays and a costume room, all set in the 16th century Guildhall.

East of England Birds of Prey Centre is open daily 10.30am to 5.30pm, and there are three flying displays every day at 11.30am, 2.00 and 4pm.

This is a conservation centre where Bengalese Eagle Owl, Peregrine Falcon, Snowy Owl and many more exotic birds of Prey are housed.

Laxfield Baptist Church bears a plaque to the memory of John Noyes, burnt at the stake in September 1557 for refusing to becoming a Catholic. The villagers, with one exception, doused their domestic fires in protest, and the one fire which still burned was used to light the stake.

The *King's Head* is a 15th century pub with no bar, where beer is served straight from kegs in the cellar. The pub has lots of character and atmosphere with low ceilings, long passages and old wooden seats. Bar meals are home-made and the soups are great. Take a ride in a Horse and Carriage around the beautiful countryside and stop at the pub for lunch, where rides can be arranged.

Turn left and left again through country lanes to Cratfield.

Cratfield

St Mary's Church is an impressive flint building with a fine chancel roof, and has one of the finest rings of six bells.

Pass through Huntingfield onto the B1117, then turn right.

Heveningham

Heveningham Hall, a Georgian mansion built in the 18th century, overlooks beautiful grounds, the lake and the River Blyth.

> Pass through Ubbeston Green on the B1117. Turn left through country lanes, then take the second right onto the B1118 and pass through Brundish. At the 'T' intersection, turn right, then right again onto the A1120.

Dennington

Very pretty little village where the post office is recorded as being one of the oldest in the country and has been in the same building since 1830.

The *Queens Head*, built in the late 1600s, is a lovely pub with great atmosphere.

The *Church of St Mary* was built in the 14th century and is the resting place of Lord Bardolph, who was buried here in the 15th century.

The 15th century screens, complete with lofts and parapets, and the 14th century carved chancel windows and carved pews are some of the best in Suffolk.

> Leave on the A1120, then take the third road on the right and pass through Saxtead. Take the third right again.

Monk Soham

Church of St Peter has a very wide five light chancel window, a 15th century seven-sacrament font, and an iron banded chest dating from the 14th century that is over 8ft long. The Stuart Holy Table is beautifully carved.

> Turn second right and pass through Kenton onto the B1077, then turn left.

Debenham

This is really a fantastic village and well worth a visit. The river Deben runs beside the main street, and meanders in and out of the village. There are many picturesque timber-framed buildings dating from the 14th century.

The *Cherry Tree* pub has fabulous windows with little squares.

The *Church of St Mary* has a magnificent west porch, 15th century nave, and parts of the tower are pre-Norman. The church base has been described as the finest piece of Saxon work in Suffolk.

Craft Centres: *Carters Kiln & Cottage Pottery*, Low Road, ph (01728) 860 475. One of Britain's top teapot makers, has a lovely collection of novelty teapots and is open all year.

Continue on the B1077.

Winston

Very small village with a church and a few cottages. The scenery all around here is postcard material, because hedges, fields, and the soil are different colours.

Drive onto the A1120, then turn right .

Pettaugh

Very pretty little village with charming cottages where St Catherine's Church was once served by the monks of Leiston Abbey.

Continue on the A1120.

Stonham Aspal

The village was named after Robert de Aspal who was rector in 1294. The church has a wooden top to the tower which houses 10 bells.

The *Ten Bells Inn* offers a very warm welcome. The pub takes its name from the church's bells.

Craft Centres: *Stonham Barns* on Pettaugh Road, ph (01449) 711 755. Open all year has rural craft workshops, pets' corner, and the *Farmer's Table* restaurant provides very generous servings of home-made cooking.

Golf: *Stonham Barns Golf Driving Range*, ph (01449) 711 060. Custom built range with all weather bays plus bunker shot and putting green practice area.

Turn left onto the A140.

Earl Stonham

The village is scattered around three greens, Middlewood Green, Forward Green and Broad Green.

St Mary's Church is 13th century and has a magnificent carved roof and wall paintings.

Craft Centres: *Ascot House Crafts* is well worth a visit for its 1000 sq ft of attractive pottery, collectables and other items.

Turn left onto the B1078.

Coddenham

The little village lies sheltered by surrounding hills and dates from Roman times. Many archaeological finds have been made in the Baylham House area, the original site of the town. The village is unspoilt and has beautiful Suffolk pink timber-framed 15th century houses, a post office that dates from 1500 and a vicarage from the 18th century.

St. Mary's Church dates from Norman times and has many wonderful features including a large Italian painting of Christ, a 15th century Crucifixion carving, and a stone bell turret.

Take the first road on the right.

Claydon

The river Gipping runs through the village, and horse-drawn barges once went through the locks near the little humped-back bridge.

The *Crown*, has a restaurant, good bar meals, garden and play equipment for children.

Turn left.

Barham

Barham Manor is Tudor and has octagonal chimneys. Opposite the walled entrance to the former Barham Hall is 13th century *St Mary's Church*. One of the windows in the vestry is 16th century and there is a brass dated 1514. The church now serves both Barham & Claydon and is now known as St Mary and St Peter.

Shrubland Hall, in the beautiful grounds of the Park, was built in 1770 by James Paine and is now a health resort.

Henley

Very pretty little village with a little shop and a couple of lovely thatched cottages.

The *Church of St Peter* dates back to 1300 and stands in the centre of the village, from where five roads branch out. In 1848 a vestry was added to the church as a schoolroom, and the playground was the graveyard until the present school was built in 1875.

Head south to Westerfield through beautiful country roads which are well sign posted.

Westerfield

The *Church of St Mary Magdalene* has a superb single hammerbeam roof, and where the wall posts meet the ends of the hammerbeams there are angels with outstretched wings. The church has a memorial to a Major J R Whitefoord who, having successfully survived the Napoleonic Wars, was accidentally killed by a friend while out shooting. Another plaque is to Henry M Cautley, one of Westerfield's best known citizens and son of a former rector, whose books on Norfolk and Suffolk churches are standard works of reference.

The *Swan Inn* is very hospitable and the interior is delightful with lots of plates on welsh dressers, other memorabilia from the past, and lots of swan pictures and ornaments. The five rooms are beautifully divided by wood panelling and stained glass. Children are well catered for.

Return to Ipswich.

TOUR 7

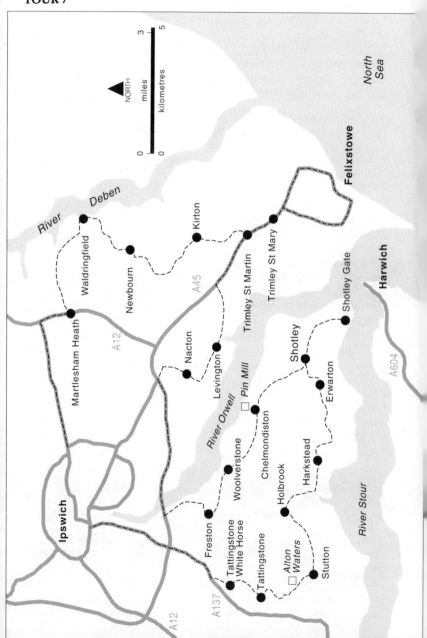

Tour 7 - Ipswich to Felixstowe

Leave Ipswich on the A12, heading east.

Martlesham Heath

An unusual village built in 1975, and converted from an RAF base. The airfield and runways have since been covered with gorse and heather. It must have taken some time disposing of the concrete, bits of aircraft and other artillery. The village has won an award for its design of individual hamlets around a village green.

The village pub is named after Sir Douglas Bader who was stationed here in 1940 to 1941 with the 242 squadron. Douglas Bader was an ace fighter pilot who lost both legs during a mission in World War II. The movie *Reach for the Sky* and a book of the same title, tell the courageous story of the man. The car park and forecourt of the pub are part of the original runway.

Country Walks: There are many interesting walks around the village and up along the coastline.

Nature Reserves: A natural area has been set aside for the silver studded blue butterfly.

Turn right off the A12.

Waldringfield

Delightful little rural village set in 190 acres of tidal river, salt marsh and foreshore. The estuary is one of the most beautiful in eastern England.

Cruises: *Waldringfield Boat Yard*, ph (01473) 736 260. The *Jahan* cruises on the River Deben from May to October at 11.30am, 2.30pm and 6.30pm.

Continue south to Newbourn.

Newbourn

St Mary's Church is the heart of this lovely little village and the Domesday Book records it as being here in 1086. The plain glass window incorporates a piece of stained glass showing the face of Christ which was recovered intact when a hurricane blew out the rest of the stained glass window.

The *Fox Inn* dates back to the 16th century and most of the old beams came from sailing ships.

The Newbourne Giants were brothers both seven feet, seven inches tall and were attractions at local fairs. They are both buried in the churchyard.

Turn left and pass through Kirton, then turn left onto the A45.

Felixstowe

Felixstowe lies in a gently curving bay between the estuaries of the rivers Deben and Orwell. Its beach, a mixture of shingle, pebbles and sand, is about 2 miles long.

Information Centre: Leisure Centre, Undercliff Road West, ph (01394) 276 770.

Hospital: Felixstowe General Hospital, Constable Road.

Police: 32 High Street.

Places To See

Martello Tower, Promenade, was built about 1810 as a defence against an invasion by Napoleon.

Landguard Fort & Museum is open end May to end September on Wednesday, Thursday & Sunday from 2.30 to 5pm. Guided tours of the Fort on Wednesday & Sunday at 2.45 & 4pm.

The 16th century Fort is on the long narrow peninsula of shingle which protects the harbour entrance. The Museum houses artefacts illustrating early 18th century history.

Church of St Peter and St Paul, founded in the 11th century, was a Benedictine priory of St Felix.

Golf: *Felixstowe Ferry Golf Club*, ph (01394) 286 834. 18 hole seaside links. Visitors are welcome after 10.30am.

Cruises: *Orwell and Harwich Navigation*, Harwich Quay. Cruises on the Orwell and Stour estuaries.

Return to the A45, then take the first on the left.

Trimley St Mary and Trimley St Martin

Twin villages, with two churches in one churchyard reputedly built by two feuding sisters.

Thomas Cavendish was born in *Grimston Hall* in 1560, and in 1592 was the second man to circumnavigate the world. The village sign depicts both him and an inscription bearing the words 'My God, said Thomas Cavendish, whatever may befall, I'll love dear Trimley and the oaks of Grimston Hall'! The *Mariners Inn* in St Mary's has a painting outside showing Cavendish's three ships.

Nature Reserves: *Trimley Marshes*. Grazing marsh, reed bed and wetland created from former farmland, with wildfowl, waders and migrants, and plant life. Access on foot from the car park in Station Road, Trimley St Mary.

Back onto the A45, then turn left.

Levington

Pretty village on the banks of the River Orwell, where St Peter's Church overlooks the river. Levington Hall was the Squire's residence and the lodge cottage was where the gardener lived.

The *Ship Inn* is an old smugglers' haunt and is still a favourite retreat where the *locals* meet to relax over a pint and enjoy an excellent meal.

Nacton

The Church of St Martin, Orwell Park House and Broke Hall all date from 1200.

Colonel George Tomline, an engineer, lived at Orwell Park House and owned most of the area between the Orwell and the Deben. In 1850 he had the village moved to its present site, and he also built a school at Seven Hills, and the railway line from Ipswich to Felixstowe.

Turn left onto the A45. Turn left over the river Orwell, onto the B1080, then take the second turn right.

Freston

The village on the river Orwell has been in existence since the 8th century and has some wonderful old buildings, including Bond Hall a lovely 16th century Manor House. *Boot Inn* and the Old Forge are both 17th century, and Monkey Lodge, Latimer Cottage and Tudor Tower are all 18th century.

Cross the B1080, onto the B1456.

Woolverstone

Hamlet on the river Orwell has been here since the Bronze Age, and legend has it that a Viking marauder by the name of Wulf sacrificed a maiden on a huge stone, giving the village its name.

Woolverstone Hall was built in 1776.

Woolverstone House School, once known as St Peter's Home for Fallen Women, was run by an order of nuns. It was designed and built by Sir Edwin Lutyens, the famous architect, who was born in London in 1869 and died in 1944.

Continue along the B1456.

Cheldmondiston and Pin Mill

Village and hamlet on the river Orwell where grain and coal were once carried by large steamboats which would have been moored in Butterman's Bay. Pin Mill is now a wonderful sailing area and beauty spot.

The *Butt and Oyster* has been around since 1553. It is a must-see, especially when the tide is high and the water laps against the walls of this delightful pub.

Shotley and Shotley Gate

The *Bristol Arms,* in Shotley Gate, is a 16th century pub situated at the end of the peninsula that offers great views of the River Stour and ocean going ships. Fresh home-made fish dishes are a speciality with very generous servings at very reasonable prices. The forecourt overlooking the quay is a popular place to eat in the summer.

Shotley is made up of several hamlets all mentioned in the Domesday Book in 1086.

Return to Shotley, and after passing through the village take the road to the left.

Erwarton

A small hamlet on the river Stour where Anne Boleyn visited an aunt, both as a child and as Queen of England. In a vault under the organ of the Lady Chapel in the local church there is a lead casket that supposedly contains her heart. She had apparently requested that her heart be buried here in Erwarton.

Harkstead

A pretty little village that overlooks the sea and cliffs, and was mentioned in the Domesday Book in 1086 by William the Conqueror. The 14th century *Church of St Mary* is built of flint and brick.

Holbrook

A larger-than-most village with a brook at the bottom of the hill running past the mill, and through meadows to join the River Stour at Holbrook Creek.

All Saints' Church contains an effigy of Judge John Clench, who was the first Recorder of Ipswich, dated 1607. *Clench House* was named after him and is now a home for the elderly.

Turn left onto the B1080.

Stutton

One of Suffolk's long villages mentioned in the Domesday Book in 1086 as where Stutton Hall, Crepping Hall, Alton Hall, Crowe Hall, the Rectory and Argents were all manor houses. The cottages and the street are delightful and well worth stopping for a stroll.

Boat Hire: *Alton Water Sports Centre*, Holbrook Road, Stutton, ph (01473) 328 408. Hire of wind surfers and sailing dinghies. Summer training courses and day memberships are available. Open April to October.

Bicycle Hire: *Alton Cycle Hire*, Alton Water, ph (01473) 328 873. Hire by the hour or day, tandems are also available.

Turn left off the B1080.

Alton Waters

One of Suffolk's beautiful lakes offering a great day out filled with activities that include walks, sailing, windsurfing, bird watching and coarse fishing.

Turn right onto the A137, then turn right again.

Tattingstone and Tattingstone White Horse

A village that has been here since the 6th century, and was mentioned in the Domesday Book in 1086 when it had three Anglo-Saxon manors.

The road to the *White Horse*, once a very busy coaching inn and now on the edge of the reservoir, would have been lost if Lemon Hill Bridge had not been built to access it.

Return to Ipswich on the A137.

TOUR 8

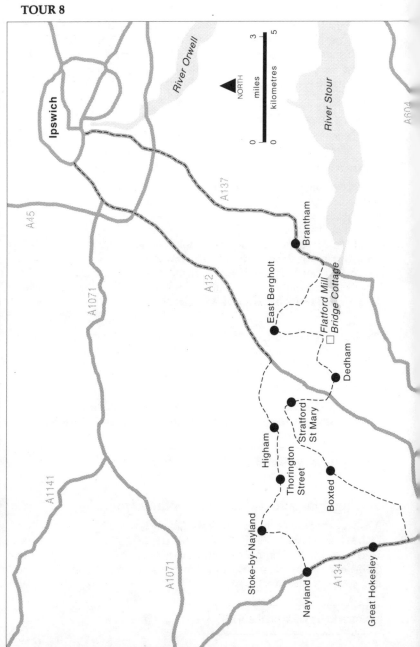

Tour 8 - Ipswich to Constable Country

Travel south on the A12, then turn right onto the B1068.

Higham

Attractive little village with a delightful little bridge over the River Brett. The countryside all around here is very picturesque and the views are magnificent.

Continue on the B1068 to Thorington Street.

Thorington Street

A pretty little village, Thorington Hall is Elizabethan, and the *The Rose* is a lovely inn painted in Suffolk pink.
Thorington Mill, at the bottom of the hill, is being restored.
Weylands Farm, owned by Roger & Cheryl Clark, is home to the beautiful *Suffolk Punches*. These horses still plough the land and are sold all over the world.

Continue along this road to Stoke-by-Nayland.

Stoke-by-Nayland

Stoke-by-Nayland is one of the landscape painter Constable country villages, and has many lovely buildings.
The *Guildhall* dates from the 1500s, and is now three private dwellings.
Black Horse Inn is a lovely timber framed building.
Tendring Hall, built during the 15th century, is the home of the Rowley family, whose head was the Lord Lieutenant of Suffolk from 1974 to 1994. The present Lord Lieutenant is the Right Honourable Lord Belstead.
St Mary's Church has been used often in landscapes painted by John Constable. There are some interesting tombs and brasses in the church which is not open on wet days.
The Angel Inn, in the village centre, has a very comfortable 17th century interior, and a charming cosy lounge divides the two bars from the dining room. One of the bars has an ancient 40ft well. Excellent meals, very reasonably priced, are served.

> Turn left onto the B1087.

Nayland

In the High Street is the lovely 15th century *Alston Court*, with mullioned window, panelled front door and canopied hood. The *Guildhall* is also 15th century and overlooks the square.

Abels Bridge was originally built of wood in the 15th century and divided Essex from Suffolk. In the 16th century a hump bridge was built to allow barges to navigate the river. It was renovated in 1959, and the keystone transferred from the old bridge bears the letter *A* and a bell.

The beautiful *Church of St James* was the second church to be built on the site in 1400. One of the two Constable religious paintings hangs in the church. The other is in the *Church of St Michael* in Brantham.

> Leave the village on the A134, heading south. Pass through Great Hokesley, turn left. At the 'T' intersection turn left. Pass through Boxted.

Stratford St Mary

This is the southernmost village in Suffolk on the Essex border. The river Stour runs through the beautiful little village lying nestled in the valley of Gun Hill and Stratford Hill. The by-pass road now leaves it for the traveller to find the beautiful historic buildings here.

St Mary's Church is a very large and imposing church, well worth visiting, and dates from the 12th century.

The Anchor, is a lovely old inn.

Driving out of Stratford St Mary, opposite the *Swan Hotel*, is a stream and a pond, which has an unusual chain link fence. On the top of the poles, animals have been made from wrought iron, such as a swan and a duck.

The *Black Horse*, opposite Alderley House, is a very large old pub.

> Cross the A12.

Dedham

Dedham Vale is described as *Constable Country*, as it was this beautiful countryside which inspired him and has been immortalised in his paintings. Constable said about this area, "these scenes made me a painter".

Approaching the town on the River Stour, there are huge mansions, big houses, and lovely thatched cottages. The high street still retains original shops and buildings, and the elegant houses are mostly Tudor and Georgian.

Early Closing Day: Wednesday.
Places To See
Dedham Art & Craft Centre & Toy Museum are all open from 10am to 5pm all year. Closed Monday during January, February, March & during the Christmas period. The Toy Museum is open Tuesday, Wednesday, Thursday & Saturday & Sunday 10.30am to 4.30pm. Open Bank Holidays. Closed over lunchtimes.

The Toy Museum is in an attic setting and is a fascinating collection of toys, pictures and childhood memorabilia.
Dedham Rare Breeds Farm, Mill Street, is open every day all year from 10am to dusk, ph (01206) 322 176. Closed from mid January to the end of February.

Breeds of farm animals that are in danger of extinction can be found here, such as breeds of pigs, sheep, cattle, turkey, goats and poultry. The animals are in one acre sized paddocks divided by wide walkways.
The Sir Alfred Munnings Art Museum is open May to October on Wednesday, Sunday & Bank Holiday Monday, and Thursday & Saturday in August 2pm to 5pm.

The museum contains a collection of paintings and drawings by Sir Alfred Munnings, and is housed in *Castle House*, south of the village. The building is partly Tudor and partly Georgian, and was once the home of Sir Alfred Munnings.
The *Church of St. Mary* is most beautiful and inspiring, and was built in 1500.
The *Rose and Crown* is a lovely pub offering plenty of atmosphere and character.

Flatford

Flatford Mill is a well-preserved white cottage home that stands beside the river Stour. It was the home of Constable's friend Willy Lott, and Constable spent much of his boyhood at this mill with his family. To reach the mill, cross over the wooden bridge and walk along the tow path.

The entrance to *Gibbonsgate Field* is alongside Willy Lott's House, and is a circular walk of just under one mile with views over the Cattawade Marshes. There is a bird hide overlooking Gibbonsgate Lake.
Bridge Cottage complex includes the John Constable Exhibition, a tearoom, a shop and a restored dry dock.

Three farms comprise 330 acres of the Dedham Vale to the west and east of Dedham. The land features in several of John Constable's best known paintings. Access is on public footpaths, including the Essex Way which passes through Bridges Farm. Visit Bridge Cottage for further information on walking in this area.
Boat Hire: Hire a rowing boat on the River Stour, open from Easter to October daily.

East Bergholt

Leaving Flatford Mill and the Constable walks, you enter this delightful little village by way of very narrow one way lanes, at the end of which is a very large imposing grey mansion that was once the home of Randolph Churchill, Sir Winston's son.

St Mary's Church is one of the most inspiring churches, and has an unfinished tower that was begun in 1525. In the churchyard is the bell-house, a 16th century timber building. Inside the church is a 15th century wall painting, and a memorial glass to Constable's wife Maria. His parents are buried in the churchyard.

North of the church is The Gables, a 16th century house.

The village is a very interesting mix of houses, some dating from the 14th century. The village store also houses the Post Office, butcher and greengrocery. The *Red Lion* is a typical village pub with a very friendly welcome, and bar meals that are very good.

The *Royal Oak* has good bar meals and the garden caters for children and has ample parking.

John Constable was born here on June 11, 1776.

Turn left onto the A137.

Brantham

The *Church of St Michael* has one of the two Constable religious paintings; the other is in the church at Nayland.

Return to Ipswich on the A137.

Tour 9 - Ipswich to Southwold

Leave Ipswich heading north on the A12 and pass through Little Glemham.

Saxmundham

Lovely village has some very old and interesting shops and is well worth walking around.

The Bell Hotel in the town centre offers traditional English fare and also a variety of Mediterranean cuisine. Children are welcome in this warm and hospitable hotel.

Leave Saxmundham, heading north along the country road to Kelsale.

Kelsale

Delightful little village with lanes leading off to the hamlets of East Green, North Green and Curlew Green.

Leave the village and continue along scenic country roads, which are narrow in places. Join the B1122, turn right, then turn left onto the B1125.

Westleton

Westleton has won Suffolk's *Best Kept Village* award many times, and it's not hard to see why, with its large triangular green sloping down to the duck pond and the 18 lime trees planted for the men of the village who did not return from the first world war. Cottages cluster around the two smaller greens and along The Street. For those who are avid book collectors, a must is to visit the old chapel, now the *Robert Jackson, Chapel Books & Gallery*.

Minsmere Nature Reserve is open daily Easter to end of October from 9am to dusk. The Reserve is only a few minutes' walk away from the village, and you can discover a wealth of wildlife on the beautiful Suffolk coast. There are 2000 acres of marsh, lagoon, heath and woodland. Take a walk, it's well worth the exercise.

St Peter's Church, built by the monks from Sibton Abbey in 1340, still retains its thatched roof.

The *Crown Inn* in the centre of the village has changed very little over the years according to the photographs on the walls. There is a lovely

TOUR 9

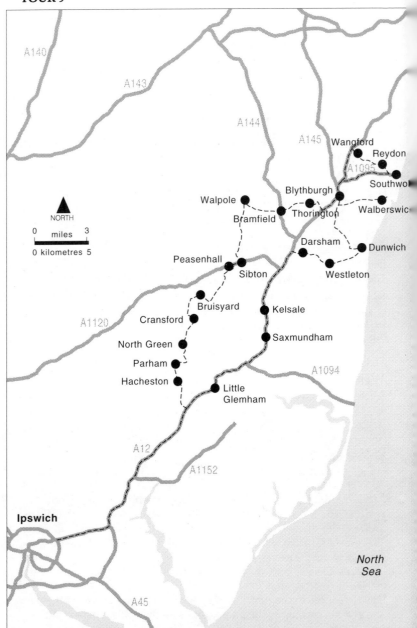

conservatory, and they have lunchtime barbecues on the weekends, weather permitting. A log fire is welcome after a long walk on colder days.

Pass through the village, then turn left.

Darsham

Bicycle Hire: *Byways Bicycles*, Priory Lane. Open daily May to October between 10am to 6pm, or by prior arrangement.
Nature Reserves: *Darsham Marshes* and acid grassy heath by the Minsmere river.

Dunwich

Dunwich Underwater Exploration Exhibition in The Craft Shop, Front Street, Orford is open all year daily 11am to 5pm. Marine archaeology and coastal erosion displays show the exploration of ruins of the former town of Dunwich which is now largely under sea.

Dunwich Heath is an inspiration to the many artists and writers who visit the 214 acres of sandy cliffs, heath and beach.

The *Museum* in St James's Street is open March on Saturday & Sunday 2pm to 4.30pm; April to September daily 11.30am to 4.30pm; and October daily 12noon to 4pm. It houses local town history from Roman times.

Greyfriars 13th century monastic remains on the cliff top should not be missed. The Leper Hospital, chapel ruins, priory and 19th century church are all that is left, yet visiting here you can relate to the history of this tiny village, once a thriving town.

The continuous erosion of the cliffs and the flooding of storms have reduced one of the East Coast's busiest towns to a handful of cottages, a beach cafe, a fishermen's hut, a pub and a general shop. Some of the houses have lattice windows and Elizabethan chimneys. At the start of the 13th century, the town had grown big enough for nine churches to be needed to serve the population.

The Ship Inn is a very popular Tudor pub lying close to the sea. The menu caters for both the restaurant and the lovely mellow bar hung with fishing nets and floats. Regulars come in for a pint of the local brew, *Adnams of Southwold*, and to eat fresh fish, simply but expertly cooked, that has travelled all of 20 yards from boat to table. The enclosed courtyard and large orchard garden are lovely.

Back towards the A12 through Dunwich Forest turn right onto B1125 then turn right onto the B1387.

Walberswick

Once a busy port, this is now a very pleasant seaside village. You can still imagine the time when the fishermen would bring their catch home, then walk up the street to their little cottages.

The local pub on the village green is very popular and within an easy walk of both the harbour and the beach.

The *Church of St Andrew* was built in the late 1600s, and stands in the ruins of a larger church that was destroyed by fire.

Country Walks: *Walberswick & Westleton Heaths*, Bird Sanctuary, where you can enjoy a good country walk on the heaths.

Return to the A12, then turn right.

Blythburgh

Small village on the River Blyth is set in very pretty countryside. On the approach into the village the magnificent spires and towers of the church dominate the landscape.

The *Church of the Holy Trinity* was built in the 15th century and is 127ft long and 54ft wide. The pillars still bear the scars of the time when Cromwell used the nave as a stable. There is a wealth of medieval treasures within the church. Open 8am to 4pm in winter and 8am to 7.30pm in summer.

Nature Reserves: *Norman Gwatkin Reserve* is a large area of marsh and fen with alder and willow coppice, walkway and 2 hides.

Craft Centres: *Blythburgh Pottery*, *Dorothy Midson Ceramics*, behind the Post Office, Chapel Road. Suffolk's smallest working pottery. Open all year 11am to 5pm.

Turn off right onto the A1095.

Southwold

A very old and elegant seaside resort which still retains bathing huts. The River Blyth to the south and Buss Creek to the north form two of the boundaries. The town has seven greens, but due to a fire in 1659 many of the original houses have been destroyed. Clusters of houses around the greens are a mixture of design, but blend well together. In 1509 The Common was given to the town and it extends into the Town Marshes and down to the River Blyth.

In 1672 the English and French fleets clashed with the Dutch just offshore in Sole Bay.

The six 18lb guns standing on the cliff were captured from the Scots at Culloden, and given to the town by the Duke of Cumberland.

The local brewery still produces a wonderful ale that they continue to deliver by horse and dray.

Information Centre: Town Hall, Market Place, ph (01502) 724 729.

Hospital: Field Stile Street.

Police: Station Road.

Annual Events: Trinity Fair in May

                      Sailing Regattas in May and August.

Places To See

The *Museum*, on Bartholomew Green, is open Easter to September daily 2.30 to 4.30pm. It has good photographs of Southwold railway, charts and pictures of the Battle of Sole Bay in 1672, and many other interesting artefacts and memorabilia.

Sailor's Reading Room, East Street, is open all year daily 9am to 5pm. Photographs, books and models connected with boats and the sea are housed here.

Lifeboat Museum, Gun Hill, is open from the end May to the end of September daily 2.30 to 4.30pm. Although small, this museum has a good collection of Royal National Life Boat Institution (RNLI) related material and models.

The *Craighurst*, on the corner on the Esplanade, is very nice and offers beautifully prepared, reasonably priced meals with generous servings.

Southwold Jack, the 15th century man-at-arms carved figure on the church, strikes the bell for services to begin in *St Edmund's Church* which dates from 1460.

The Church stands on the site of a far older church dating from 1200. The 100ft high tower stands watch over the town.

The *Crown* is an unusual combination of pub, restaurant and small hotel. Originally a coaching inn, the bars have comfortable settles and chairs set in a cheery atmosphere.

Golf: *Southwold Golf Club*, The Common, ph (01502) 723 234. 9 holes, seaside common land course. Restrictions apply.

Bicycle Hire: *E J Tooke*, 2 Blythe Road, ph (01502) 722 204. Open Easter to September from Monday to Saturday 8.30am to 5pm and Sunday 9am to 12noon.

Cruises: *Osprey* boat trips on the River Blyth. Booking information, ph (01502) 722 287, from May to September 11am to 5pm.

Leave on the B1126.

Reydon

Very pretty countryside around here. Reydon Hall is an Elizabeth Manor, and St Margaret's Church was recorded in the Domesday Book.

Wangford

The Church of St Peter and St Paul is Perpendicular, and has one very interesting tower. The original tower was removed in 1865 and when the new tower was built it was placed at the eastern end instead of the usual western end. The church was built on the site of a priory for Cluniac monks.

There are a number of very old buildings in this lovely little village including the *Vicarage* which dates from the early 18th century and *Well Cottage* from 1755.

Country Walks: *Henham Walks*. There are two walks of 1¼ miles and 5 miles of waymarked paths through Repton Park, lake and woods. See wildlife, highland cattle and rare breed sheep or just have a picnic. Open all year 10am to 6pm.

> Turn left onto the A12 and pass through Blythburgh, then take the second right. Pass through Thorington.

Bramfield

The thatched church with a detached round tower has a lovely rood screen. Bramfield House, a Boys' Home, is just one of the lovely houses that make up this very pretty little village.

Walpole

Lovely little village with delightful houses and buildings, set on the River Blyth in fabulous countryside.

> Turn left on the B1117 and turn immediate left.

Sibton

Very pretty cluster of little cottages, a small 18th century bridge, and the *White Horse*, the only pub in the village. Ruins, now overgrown, are all that remain of Sibton Abbey, the only Cistercian house in Suffolk, founded in 1150.

> Turn right onto the A1120.

Peasenhall

Houses are clustered on the banks of a gently trickling stream which runs through the village. The village shop has been run by the same family for over three generations and holds a Royal Warrant for pickled ham using a secret family recipe. The *Swan Inn* is a very popular pub.

Turn left.

Bruisyard

Wine: *Bruisyard Vineyard & Herb Centre*, Church Road, ph (01728) 638 281. Open daily New Year to Christmas from 10.30am to 5pm. Admission to the vineyard is free, a charge is made for the tour. This establishment is the producer of the award winning *Bruisyard St Peter* wine in a 10 acre vineyard with its own winery. There is a restaurant and shop where its own and other East Anglian wines can be bought. Enjoy a stroll through the herb and water gardens or just have a picnic.

Pass through Cransford. Turn right after leaving the village. Cross the B1119 and pass through North Green.

Parham

Parham Airfield is home to the *390th Bomb Group Memorial Air Museum*, which is open March to October on Sunday 11am to 6pm.

The collection reflects East Anglia's involvement in aviation during World War II. Housed in a 1942 control tower of the former USAAF bomber base, the exhibits include engines and artefacts from many famous aircraft, and uniforms and memorabilia relating to the RAF, the US 8th Air Force and the German Air Force.

The Library and Archives Centre are located in a Nissen hut.

Pass through Hacheston back onto the A12 and return to Ipswich.

TOUR 10

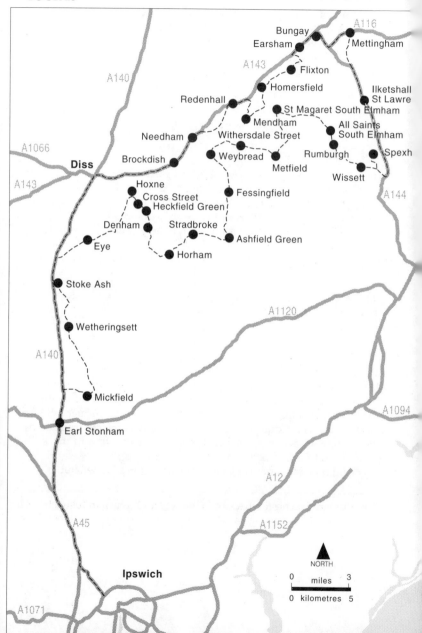

Bungay
A116
Earsham
Mettingham
A143
Flixton
A140
Homersfield
Ilketshall
St Lawre
Redenhall
St Magaret South Elmham
South Elmham
A1066
Mendham
All Saints
Needham
Withersdale Street
South Elmham
Brockdish
Weybread
Rumburgh
Spexh
A143
Metfield
Wissett
Diss
A144
Hoxne
Fessingfield
Cross Street
Heckfield Green
Denham
Stradbroke
Eye
Ashfield Green
Horham
Stoke Ash
A1120
A1094
Wetheringsett
A140
Mickfield
Earl Stonham
A45
A12
A1152
Ipswich
A1071

NORTH

0   miles   3

0   kilometres   5

Tour 10 - Ipswich to Bungay

> Drive north on the A45, turn right onto the A140 and pass through Earl Stonham. Turn right and pass through Mickfield and Wetheringsett, then take the second on the left.

Stoke Ash

Colsey Wood House was at one time a large H-shaped house with a moat and fish ponds, and was a Benedictine convent. Legend has it that it was once joined to *Wood Hall*.

Wood Hall Manor was first recorded in 1206 and has a moat dating from the late 1300s, but the present house is dated 1600.

> Turn right onto the A140, then turn right for Eye.

Eye

A fascinating town with character. Beautiful old houses, antique and interesting shops make up this lovely 18th century market town.
Police: Victoria Road.
Early Closing Day: Tuesday.
Places To See
The remains of a *Norman Castle* dated from 1156 are worth seeing, and there are great views of the town and the surrounding countryside from the top.
The Pennings is a lovely picnic spot and wildlife area.
Linden House, in Lambeth Street, is dated 1750.
The Guildhall dates from 1470 and stands between the church and the primary school, once the grammar school.
The *Church of St Peter and St Paul* was founded in the 12th century has a rood screen dating from 1470 and a magnificent 100ft tower which dominates the landscape. Open daily 7.15am to 6.30pm.
Golf: *Diss Golf Club*, Stuston, ph (01379) 622 847. 18 holes and restrictions apply.

> Leave the town heading east on the B1177, then turn left.

Hoxne

The magnificent 13th century *Church of St Peter and St Paul* still holds Harvest Festivals, and after the service the congregation go down the hill to the village green for a full traditional breakfast.

The *Swan* in the village centre is a Suffolk Pink heavily timber fronted building with the most beautiful 15th century interior. The oak floors, beams, huge inglenook fireplaces and large wood panelled latched doors make this a real treat to visit. The food complements this delightful pub, with a large selection of excellent, reasonably priced bar meals. The garden is surrounded by shrubs and trees which extend to the banks of the river.

Turn right and pass through Cross Street and Heckfield Green.

Denham

Pretty little village where the *Church of St John* is 14th century.

Turn left.

Horham

The Norman *Church of St Mary* is on the site of a previous wooden Saxon church. The tower was strengthened to rehang the retuned peal of eight bells that is believed to be the oldest in the world.

Turn left.

Stradbroke

The village sign depicts a 12th century Bishop helping the poor. The *Town House* is a 15th century black and white timber building that was given to the village by the Lord of the Manor in 1587.

The 14th century *All Saints' Church* is in the centre of the village. The 15th century high tower shows a large star at Christmas welcoming travellers not only to church but to this very friendly village.

Turn left before Ashfield Green.

Fressingfield

The *Church of St Peter and St Paul* has a lovely stone bell turret that was built in the 14th century. The hammerbeam roof is magnificent, and fine woodwork can be seen on the nave pews which are carved with buttressed armrests and poppyheads. One pew has the initials A.P. possibly for Alice de la Pole, Duchess of Suffolk, and grand-daughter of Chaucer. Outside the south wall of the church is the tomb of an Archbishop of Canterbury who refused to take the Oath of Allegiance to William and Mary.

The *Fox and Goose Restaurant*, at one time the Guildhall, is timber framed and is a diners' delight.

Pass through Weybread and turn right onto the B1123. Pass through Withersdale Street and Metfield. Leave the village and take the turn left, then left again.

St Margaret South Elmham

A small village rambling alongside the village green, where the church is an attractive little building of Perpendicular style. The village stocks are in the porch of the church.

It is very picturesque all around here. The countryside is really lovely and although off the beaten track is well worth the drive along the narrow country lanes.

Pass through All Saints South Elmham.

Rumburgh

The *Church of St Michael and St Felix* was dedicated to the Benedictine priory founded here before the Norman conquest. The west tower dates from the 13th century and has a weatherboard top and tile pitched roof.

The *Rumburgh Buck* is a very popular pub that was once part of the church estate, where monks' guests would stay. This old building has retained its original design and still has a flagstone floor.

Continue along country roads.

Wissett

Rather a quaint little place with a nice pub called the *Plough*. *Wissett Hall* is a very large mansion and there is a cute little humpback bridge before you enter the village. Many of the buildings have oak beams that have been taken from the once heavily wooded forest nearby.

The *Church of St Andrew* has Norman features, but it also has Saxon parts.

Wine: *Wissett Wines*, Valley Farm Vineyards, is open daily all year, with tours and tastings by arrangement. Ten acre vineyard with wine sales, gardens and lovely picnic area.

Turn left and pass through Spexhall, then turn left onto the A144.

Ilketshall St Lawrence

The church is a simple 12th century building and stands on a mound reputed to be an old Roman staging post.

Wine: *The Cider Place*, Cherry Tree Farm, Ilketshall St Lawrence, ph (01986) 781 353. Open all year 9am to 1pm & 2 to 6pm. Traditional farm brewed ciders, apple juices, country wines, mead, preserves and tastings.

Continue on the A144. Turn right before Bungay.

Mettingham

Mettingham Castle, built in 1342, is well known for its 14th century gateway and ivy clad walls, and it was here, in 1842, that six silver bells were found in the moat. The present house in the castle grounds was built in 1880.

The Norman *All Saint's Church* stands on a hill almost in the centre of the village.

The *Tally Ho* built in 1845, is a very comfortable pub serving good meals that are reasonably priced. It has a lovely collection of china jugs, teapots and plates. Children are catered for and in the garden are swings and climbing frames. There is also wheelchair access and ample parking.

Bungay

Bungay, a market town and yachting centre on the river Waveney, has lovely Georgian houses set in and around the market place, which is of architectural significance.

Remains of the original Norman Castle, built in 1165, are open daily 9am to 6pm. There are twin towers and massive flint walls, and a tunnel supported by timbers that could be removed when attack threatened. This would cause the entire corner of the building to collapse on the invaders.

Museum, Council Office, Broad Street, is open all year Monday to Friday from 9am to 1pm & 2pm to 4.30pm. It consists of two small rooms of artefacts.

The *Church of St Mary* was once a church of the Benedictine nuns founded in the 12th century. The tower, built at the end of the 15th century, has remarkable buttresses and turrets.

The *Church of Holy Trinity* contains a fine pulpit, dating from 1558, and a monument.

In the market place stands the *Butter Cross* (Market Cross), erected in 1869 after the fire of 1866 which destroyed so much of the town. The dome was added in 1754 and has a fine statue of Justice.

The *White Lion* pub stands in part of the old castle site.

The *Chequers Inn* in Bridge Street, is a 16th century pub serving good home-cooked meals. The atmosphere, friendliness and warm welcome are like those of a village pub. The exposed beams have dozens of beer jugs hanging from them, and the dark oak chairs, traditional benches, bar stools and half panelled walls make this a very cosy pub. Children are catered for with an outdoor play area.

Golf: *Bungay & Waveney Valley*, Outney Common, ph (01986) 892 337. 18 holes course with natural features. Restrictions apply.

Boat Hire: *Outney Meadow Caravan Park*, ph (01986) 892 338. Explore the Upper River Waveney by Canadian canoes, kayaks and rowing boats, from Easter to October daily.

Leave on the A143 for Earsham.

Earsham

The village, surrounded by rolling countryside, is mainly farmland, and was mentioned in the Domesday Book.

The Otter Trust is open April to October daily 10.30am to 6pm. It is the largest collection of otters in natural enclosures where the British Otter is bred for re-introduction to the wild. Situated on the banks of the River Waveney, there are also unique collections of waterfowl, night heron and deer.

Three lakes with riverside walks set in lovely surroundings are well worth the stroll.

All Saints' Church is believed to stand on a Roman site, but is mainly 14th century although part of the nave is supposedly Norman.

Earsham Hall lies on the outskirts of the village. The main part was built in 1710, but it is thought that a previous Hall existed on the same site.

Country Walks: Walks in and around Waveney range from 2½ miles to 10 miles. There are five country walks of varying distances around Mutford, Dunwich, Blundeston, Beccles and the Faiths.

Take the by-pass road.

Flixton

This pretty woodland village is named after St Flik, the first East Anglian Bishop. The village sign, erected in 1921, depicts the Bishop.

Norfolk & Suffolk Aviation Museum, on the B1062 Homersfield Road, is open April to October on Sunday 10am to 5pm. There are 17 historic aircraft and other aviation material including the 446th Bomb Group Museum and Memorial and the Royal Observer Corps Museum.

The church, mainly Victorian, is an unusual shape, but the site dates back to 700AD.

The *Buck Inn*, is a popular pub for those visiting the aircraft collection.

Homersfield

A picturesque little village with some thatched cottages around the village green, overlooked by St Mary's Norman Church.

The *Black Swan*, on the banks of the River Waveney, where the policy of 'freshly caught, locally bought and home-made' applies, is a delightful, warm and hospitable pub. There are four bars serving meals and an elegant dining room. Children are welcome and the large garden has barbecues in the summer. Take a walk on the riverside and through the meadows, it's well worth it.

Mendham

Pretty little village on the river Waveney, where Sir Alfred Munnings the painter was born in 1878.

Turn left out of the village then right.

Redenhall

St Mary's Church was built between 1460 and 1520 and has a 120ft high Perpendicular tower. The octagonal font, unique double headed brass lectern dating from 1500, and the wooden eagle lectern make this a very interesting church to visit.

Drive onto the A143 and pass through Needham and Brockdish, then turn left onto the A140 and return to Ipswich.

TOUR 11

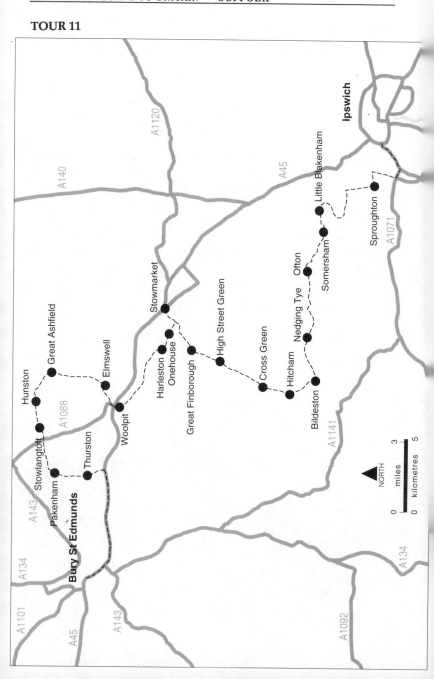

Tour 11 - Ipswich to Bury St Edmunds

Take the road to Chantry, turn right onto the A45, then turn left.

Sproughton

The village sign on the green depicts the mill and the legendary Wild Man. Sproughton has been in existence for many centuries, and during excavations many Neolithic/Bronze Age artefacts have been discovered.

The town boasts a *Mill* and a *Mill House*. The picturesque house dates from the 1600s, and the 18th century mill, last used for milling in 1947, has attracted many artists.

The *Church of All Saints* dates from the 1200s, and the 16th century rectory stands nearby.

Sproughton Hall is 17th century and the tithe barn of the same era was handed to the villagers in 1978. It has been restored and is now the local sports and recreation hall.

The *almshouses* in Lower Street were originally built in 1634, and rebuilt in 1876.

Turn left.

Little Blakenham

The town's main attraction is the *Blakenham Woodland Garden*, ph (01473) 830 344. Open March 1 to June 30, Sunday to Friday 1pm to 5pm. There is an admission charge, free parking and no dogs are allowed in the gardens. It is a 5 acre garden with many rare trees and shrubs. Especially lovely in the spring with ·bluebells, camellias and magnolias, followed in the summer by roses.

Somersham

The approach is along the brook which runs through the village to the river Gipping. The village dates back to the 5th century and was once a Saxon settlement. Wonderful old houses line the street and the village sign shows that horses were a very important aspect of village life. There is a blacksmith's anvil in the garden of Forge Bungalow.

St Mary's Church is Saxon and was mentioned in the Domesday Book in 1086. It is now mainly 14th century but still retains an arch in the porch that is reputed to be the oldest in the country.

The *Duke of Marlborough*, with its tales of being haunted, is surrounded by some of the oldest houses in the village. The house opposite the pub has a *pudding stone*, which was to stop carts from damaging the walls.

> Leave the village and take the second road on the left and pass through Offton. At the 'T' intersection turn left onto the B1078. Pass through Nedging Tye.

Bildeston

The village has many delightful timber-framed cottages with overhanging upper storeys. The market place is 19th century and the clock tower is Victorian.

The *Church of St Mary* was built in the 15th century and stands on a hill at the end of the village. The wonderful carved door and hammerbeam roof are worth seeing.

The *Red Lion* has good meals both at the bar and in the restaurant. The garden is nice and has a play area.

The *Crown Hotel* in the village centre is a 15th century Suffolk Pink pub with timbered front and leaded windows. The interior has been restored to its former glory with huge inglenooks, cosy bar, restaurant and beautifully furnished bedrooms. Bar meals and Ploughman's lunches served at the bar are delightful and reasonably priced, as are restaurant meals. The large secluded garden is lovely.

> At Hitcham, turn right onto the B1115. Pass through Cross Green and High Street Green.

Great Finborough

The Victorian *Church of St Andrew* has a spire that dominates the landscape and was rebuilt in 1875. The medieval porch is the only part of the original building that remains.

Stowmarket

An historic market town on the A1308, 12 miles north-west of Ipswich, Stowmarket is set in the delightful Gipping Valley. It is well worth a visit to stroll around the interesting buildings and shops.

Information Centre: Wilkes Way, ph (01449) 676 800.
Doctors' Surgery: Health Centre, Violet Hill Road.
Police: Violet Hill Road.
Market Days: Thursday and Saturday.
Early Closing Day: Tuesday.

Places To See

Abbot's Hall and the *Museum of East Anglian Life*, ph (01449) 612 229, is open daily March to October from 10am to 5.30pm.

Abbot's Hall Manor, dating from 1284, belonged to the monks of St Osyth. The site of an old monastery, it is now privately owned.

The Museum occupies 70 acres and since opening in 1967, many new buildings complement the 13th century Abbot's Hall Barn, 18th century working watermill, smithy, and 14th century farmhouse. There are demonstrations of traction engines and other equipment and the animals, riverside walks, shop and picnic areas make a visit a great way to spend a day.

The *Church of St Peter and St Mary* was once two churches, but the smaller St Mary's was demolished in the 16th century.

Tot Hill House Restaurant is a charming 16th century restored timber-framed house on the Bury Road, and the meals are delightful.

Golf: *Stowmarket Golf Club*, Lower Road, Onehouse, ph (01449) 736 473. 18 holes in undulating parkland. Restrictions apply at weekends.

Town Walks: take a pleasant walk along the tow path of the lovely river to Gipping.

Take the west road.

Onehouse

Onehouse Hall was once the home of Master James Rivett and was supposedly visited by Queen Elizabeth I in 1578.

St John the Baptist Church has records dating from 1312, but its origins pre-date the Norman Conquest. The nave is original and the two bells are dated 1604. The round tower is original Anglo-Saxon which is rare in Suffolk.

The *Shepherd & Dog* pub is set in beautiful rural countryside and offers inexpensive meals and lunchtime specials.

Harleston

A small, very attractive town on the River Waveney that has two market places and is now a busy commercial area. Georgian houses, the 1873 clock tower, the Corn Exchange built in 1849, and the *Swan Hotel* are all interesting buildings.

Thatch-roofed *St Augustine's Church* was probably built as a chapel for Harleston Hall. The windows are Early English and the turret houses one bell. There is no electricity in the church.

Continue through to Woolpit.

Woolpit

The village boasts a lovely little green, with an old coaching inn. The white brick from Woolpit was once very widely used, but the brickworks were closed after the second world war.

Woolpit Bygones Museum, The Street, is open April to September on Saturday & Sunday from 2.30 to 5pm.

The Museum depicts the life of a Suffolk village and has a brick-making display.

The 12th century flint *Church of St Mary* dominates the village centre. The tower and spire are 19th century. The porch is very large and the nave roof is decorated with angel carvings.

Lady's Well spring waters were believed to be a cure in 14th century.

Cross the A45 onto the A1088, then turn right.

Elmswell

St John the Baptist is a most impressive and imposing church on a hill at the entrance to this small village, overlooking Woolpit and the surrounding countryside.

Great Ashfield

This is a lovely, friendly and unspoilt little village with a cluster of houses and two pubs. One of the pubs, the *Hovell Arms*, was used by the American servicemen who were stationed nearby during the second world war. The now disused airfield was in the front line as Home Defence Air Station from September 1917 to November 1918, and was the headquarters of the 385th Bombardment Group, USAF, from June 1943 to August 1945. In the churchyard is a memorial to the Americans who died during the second world war and inside the church is a memorial altar, and a parchment roll recording the names of those who failed to return from their bombing missions.

The 13th century *Church of All Saints* stands on an earlier site recorded in the Domesday Book in 1086. King Edmund, killed by the Danes, is supposed to have been buried here in 903AD and a Saxon Cross made from Barnack stone was erected to commemorate the event. The cross, replaced in the 19th century, now stands in Ashfield House garden.

Turn left and pass through Hunston and Stowlangtoft, then cross the A1088.

Pakenham

The village dates back to the 7th century, and forms a reversed **L** shape round a fen. It is the only village to have both a water mill and a windmill.

Pakenham Water Mill, Grimestone End, ph (01787) 247 179, is open April to September on Saturday, Sunday and Bank Holiday Monday and Wednesday from 2 to 5.30pm or by appointment. There is an admission charge. Suitable for wheelchair users.

It is a fine 18th century restored working mill, complete with oil engine and other machinery, and there are river walks, a picnic area and a shop.

Pakenham Windmill is a 19th century working tower mill.

The *Fox Inn* in the village centre, has a partly beamed bar split by an open fireplace and is a cosy place to have a bar meal. Children are welcome and the garden has a stream with ducks.

> Pass the watermill.

Thurston

The *Church of St Peter*, although rebuilt in 1860, still retains a medieval stained glass window.

> Continue on to Bury St Edmunds on the A45.

TOUR 12

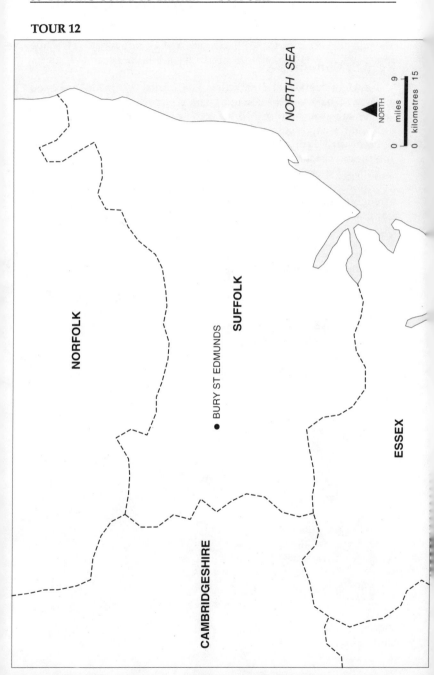

Tour 12 - Bury St Edmunds

Bury St Edmunds

The ancient market and cathedral town takes its name from the martyred Saxon king St Edmund, who was patron saint of England. His remains were brought to the local monastery 33 years after his death, at the hands of the Danes, in 870AD.

In the early 11th century the town was known as St Edmundsbury, and the monastery attained Abbey status in 1032.

Bury St Edmunds, or *Bury* as it is known locally, is very Georgian in appearance although many of the buildings and houses are older. It is a delightful and beautiful town to walk around.

Location: on the A143.

Information Centre: 6 Angel Hill, ph (01284) 764 667.

Hospital: West Suffolk Hospital, Hardwick Lane.

Police: Raingate Street.

Market Days: Wednesday and Saturday.

Early Closing Day: Thursday.

Annual Events: Cake & Ale ceremony follows the service in St Mary's Church on Thursday night after the second Monday in January. Cake, ale and a shilling are distributed to the poor of the parish.

Country Harvest Festival is held in the Cathedral in October.

Places To See

Abbey ruins and cathedral. The Abbey is one of the greatest churches in the country. What remains today is only a little of the original abbey, but it gives an idea of its former grandeur. The Norman Gate (mid-1100s), Abbey Gate (mid-1400s) and the Norman Tower are all interesting contrasts.

Gershom-Parkington collection of clocks and watches, Angel Corner, one of the largest collections in Britain, is located on the north side of the square in the Queen Anne mansion.

Market Cross Art Gallery, Cornhill, is open Tuesday to Saturday from 10.30am to 4.30pm. The building was designed by Robert Adam in 1771.

Moyses Hall Museum, Cornhill, is open all year Monday to Saturday from 10am to 5pm. Built in 1180, it is claimed to be the oldest Norman house in East Anglia with stone vaulting. The museum houses and exhibits Bronze age weapons, a 13th century monks' chronicle, Anglo-Saxon remains from West Stow and many other interesting historical items.

Suffolk Regiment Museum, The Keep, Out Risbygate Street, is open Monday to Friday 10am to 12 & 2pm to 4pm. Military uniforms, weapons, medals, photographs and many other historical pieces of the Suffolk & Cambridgeshire regiments dating from the 17th century, are on display.

St Mary's Church is 15th century with a magnificent Perpendicular exterior and has a stone pendant in the roof of the Porch. Mary Tudor, the sister of King Henry VIII is buried in the chancel. The chancel is open Monday to Saturday from 11am to 3pm in summer.

The Angel Hotel is where Charles Dickens' hero Mr Pickwick stayed when visiting the town.

Nutshell Pub is one of the smallest pubs in Britain, measuring about 16ft by 10ft. It has a lovely collection of Victorian bric-a-brac.

Manor House Museum, Honey Hill, is open daily Monday to Saturday from 10am to 5pm & Sunday 2 to 5pm. It is a fine Georgian mansion housing ceramics, costumes, paintings, furniture and many other period pieces.

Greene King Brewery Tours, ph (01284) 764 667. Open all year Monday at 2.30 and Tuesday to Thursday at 2pm.

Pentecostal Church, Churchgate Street. This Unitarian chapel has an outstanding 1711 double-decker pulpit.

St James Church, south of the Norman gate is now the cathedral church. Built in the 16th century, it has some 19th century additions.

Angel Hill has many fine buildings from the 17th and 18th centuries.

Cupola House, built in 1693, was once occupied by Daniel Defoe, author of *Robinson Crusoe*.

The *Guildhall*, built in the 12th century, was remodelled in the 19th century.

The *Linden Tree* has a fine menu and the fare is reasonably priced in the two bars and in the restaurant. One bar is very inviting with dark furniture, open fire, and bay windows. The other bar has furniture arranged on a platform with a banister rail, and the room is full of pictures, ornaments, and a great selection of bottles. Children are welcome and there is an outdoor play area.

The *Mason's Arm*, in the centre of town, dates back to 1731 and is a classical weatherboard pub serving good food and great fresh seafood. Parking is difficult, but it is an easy walk from the town centre.

Golf: *Bury St Edmunds Golf Club*, Tut Hill. 18 holes, undulating parkland course, 6615 yards, par 72. 9 hole course available Monday to Saturday inclusive. Restrictions apply at weekends.

Country Walks: *Nowton Park*, Nowton Road. 172 acres including woodland, copses, and magnificent trees. The park has a picnic area and is open daily 9am to dusk.

Horringer

The village green is dominated by the flint stone *Church of St Leonard*. Adkins Woods form an attractive background to the thatched and tiled timber-framed cottages along one side of the street. On the other side is the old Guildhall, formerly a workhouse, then a village school, and now converted into attractive houses.

Ickworth House on the A143, two miles south of Bury St Edmunds, ph (01284) 735 270. The House is open April to October on Tuesday, Wednesday, Friday, Saturday & Sunday from 1.30 to 5.30pm. The Garden and Park are open all year from 7am to 7pm.

Ickworth House and Gardens were started in 1795 by the eccentric 4th Earl of Bristol and Bishop of Derry. There is an immense oval *Rotunda* with two large wings joined by curving corridors, and the largest private collection of Georgian silver and paintings by Titian and Velasquez. There are also some family portraits by Gainsborough and Kauffman. Photography is allowed in the garden and parks, but not in the house, for security reasons.

The unusual *Italian Garden* to the south of the house includes lovely evergreens, the Orangery, hidden glades and a temple rose garden. The path from the Terrace Walk circles the Round Hill where Red and Fallow deer roam in the woodland park.

The *Six Bells* is a most friendly pub where the landlord will make you welcome and the atmosphere is great. The meals are excellent, the steak and kidney pie is outstanding, as are the soups, and all are very reasonably priced. Sit in one of the bars, in the conservatory or outside in the garden. Children are welcome and there is ample parking.

The *Beehive* is a red-brick and flint pub with its walls covered in creepers. The small secluded courtyard has a lovely neat little garden, and the inside of the pub is as beautiful as the outside with plenty of character. The meals are good and very reasonably priced, and children are welcome.

Craft Centres: *Horringer Crafts*. Demonstrations by local artists and craftsmen.

Country Walks: The landscaped park has 8 miles of waymarked walks.

TOUR 13

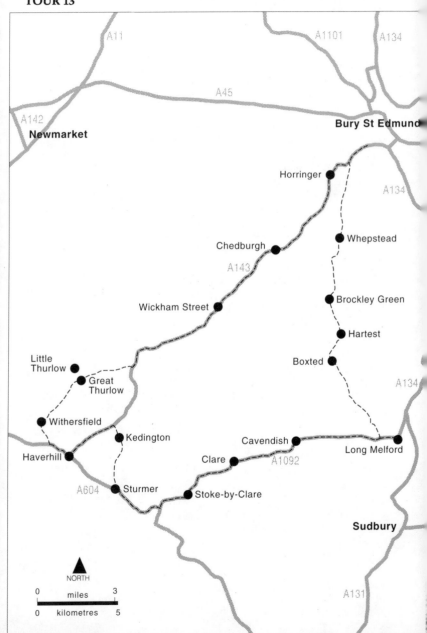

Tour 13 - Bury St Edmunds to Clare and Haverhill

Leave Bury St Edmunds on the A143 towards Horringer. Pass through the village and take the next turn left, onto the B1066.

Whepstead

Pretty little village with a church dedicated to St Petronilla, three manor houses, Plumpton Hall, Doveden Hall and the red brick half-timbered Manston Hall.

The *White Horse Inn*, about one mile from the village, is well worth the search. It was a 17th century farmhouse that became a pub in the 1800s, and has timber beams, inglenook fireplaces with fires in the winter. It offers traditional and *Mauritian* cuisine.

Brockley Green

The *Church of St Andrew* was built in the 13th and 14th centuries on a Saxon site belonging to the Abbot of St Edmunds. The tower is 16th century and in the churchyard is the base of a Tudor cross.

Hartest

Hartest has existed as a village for more than one thousand years, and on the village green stands a large glacial stone said to have been dragged there in the 1700s.

A lovely pub called the *Crown*, a beautiful village green, and really old houses add up to a very picturesque place to visit.

The *Church of All Saints* was mentioned in the Domesday Book.

Wine: *Gifford's Hall Vineyard*, ph (01284) 830 464. 12 acre vineyard with own winery open from April to end-September daily 12 noon to 6pm. Admission charge includes winery tour and wine tasting. An invitation from the owners states, *You are welcome to join us for an afternoon in the country savouring the delights of our way of life*. You will probably find them in the farm shop located in the attractively converted stable block which includes the refreshment rooms and the wine sales area. Other attractions include cut flowers, dried flowers, model organic vegetable gardens, wild flower meadows, one acre of rose gardens, rare breed Hebridean sheep, pure bred free range chickens, country walks and a picnic area.

Continue on the B1066.

Boxted

Very pretty little village with only a few cottages.

Leave the village and at the 'T' intersection, turn left onto the A1092.
Turn right onto the A134.

Long Melford

This village is situated 13 miles from Bury St Edmunds, in beautiful
South Suffolk. The heart of Long Melford is set along the impressive
one mile long and rather wide Main Street, and lies on an ancient
Roman site. Renowned for its book and antique shops and art
galleries, it is worth taking a walk up one side of the street and down
the other, exploring the mixture of Georgian and Victorian buildings
with Norfolk flat flint houses in Suffolk pink. A blue glass Roman vase
was unearthed here in 1958 and is now in the British Museum.

Annual Events: Bach Festival in Melford Hall and Holy Trinity
Church in mid-September.

Places To See

Melford Hall, ph (01787) 880 286, east of the village, lies beyond a very
imposing gateway dating from the 1550s. The Tudor Manor House has
the remains of an earlier Hall that once belonged to the Benedictine
Abbey of Bury St Edmunds.

Kentwell Hall is a magnificent red brick Tudor moated mansion, built
in 1563/4, that has an approach through one of the longest avenues of
lime trees in the country.

Kentwell Hall Home Farm, ph (01787) 310 207, is open March to October,
but you should phone for daily opening times.

Situated adjacent to the Hall, the Farm comprises a collection of
timber-framed buildings, including a 14th century aisle barn, a
granary over a cart lodge, a cow byre, a shippon for oxen, an old
fashioned pigsty, a goathouse and stables. There are also some rare
breeds including the Norfolk Horn sheep, red Tamworth pigs, British
white cattle and Suffolk Punches.

Holy Trinity Church

The 14 acre Green at the high north end of Hall Street is crowned by
the magnificent church of the Holy Trinity, built in the late 1400s on an
earlier site. The tower was added in the late 1890s. One of the most
famous churches in the country of stone and flint with nearly 100 large
windows, it is spectacular in the evenings when floodlit. Inside the
church, the nave and chancel extend over 150ft in length. The arches
and roof timbers are magnificent. Many of the monuments and brasses
are interesting as they show the style of clothing worn in the 15th

century. In the chancel is a fine memorial to Sir William Cordell, Speaker of Parliament and the master of the Rolls to Queen Elizabeth. He died in 1580, and was responsible for building the Almshouses, hospital and the magnificent Melford Hall.

The *Lady Chapel* still has mementos dating from 1669 to 1880 when it was a schoolroom. These include a children's multiplication table on one of the walls.

In the *Clopton Chantry*, is a carved memorial dedicated to John Clopton who died in 1497. The tomb is unusual as it has no effigy. The Cloptons built Kentwell Hall in 1563.

The red-brick *Almshouses* next to the church were founded in 1573 by William Cordell for twelve poor men.

Chimneys Restaurant is in a typical olde worlde building.

The *Bull Hotel* is a beautiful timbered 15th century hotel with period antiques, and exposed ceiling and wall beams. The ploughman's lunch and different types of jacket filled potatoes are definitely worth trying as a bar meal. Enjoy a lunch in the large courtyard with wrought iron furniture.

The *George & Dragon*, in the centre of the village, is a real village inn that has been lovingly restored to its 16th century glory. The bar meals are home-made from local produce, and are very reasonably priced. This really is a great place to stay while seeing the rest of Suffolk as the accommodation is excellent.

The *Hare Inn* in High Street, is Georgian but has Tudor origins. It has some great exposed oak beams and an open fire which when lit in the winter creates a very relaxing atmosphere in which to enjoy an excellent bar meal, and Suffolk beef and fish dishes are the specialties. The walled garden at the rear of the pub is very pleasant.

Country Walks: *Long Melford - Lavenham Walk.* 3 mile walk along a disused railway and farm track which links two of Suffolk's most beautiful small towns.

Leave Long Melford on the A1092.

Cavendish

This is one of Suffolk's most attractive villages, and was once the ancestral home of the Dukes of Devonshire. Thatched cottages, church and Nether Hall Farmhouse surround the green, making this a typically traditional village.

Sue Ryder Foundation Museum is open all year, daily 10am to 5.30pm, and is housed in the 16th century Rectory beside the village pond. The Rectory was used as a home for concentration camp victims. The

Museum has displays of war memorabilia, and photographs illustrating the reason for the establishment of the Foundation, and its work, past, present and future. Sue Ryder was the Founder and Social Worker of the Sue Ryder Foundation for the Sick and Disabled, Co-Founder of Mission for the Relief of Suffering, and Trustee of the Cheshire Foundation. She has received the following honours: Cross of the Order of Restitution of Poland; Medal of Yugoslav Flag with Gold Wreath and Diploma; Golden Order of Merit of Poland; OBE; CMG; Baroness Ryder of Warsaw (Life Baroness); and is the author of *And The Morrow is Theirs*.

The Sue Ryder Home, headquarters of the Sue Ryder Foundation, is the home of Lady Ryder of Warsaw and her husband Group-Captain Leonard Cheshire, VC, OM, DSO, DFC.

Pentlow Farm, on the B1064, is open from March to the end of August, Monday to Friday. It is a farm for fun and learning, where you can feed the animals or take a trailer ride. Fishing tickets are available for the day. Cafe, shop, walks and picnic area make a visit a great day out. The *Church of St Mary* has a 14th century tower that has a room with a fire-place and shuttered windows. There are two lecterns: one in brass with a 16th century brass eagle; the other in wood with two 17th century books chained to it. There are also two interesting statues, one Flemish, the other Italian. This is a very interesting church.

Wine: *Manor Vineyard*, Nether Hall, ph (01787) 280 221. A one acre vineyard that is open all year from 11am to 4pm. Charge includes a tour of the vineyard, 14th century manor house with gallery, and a museum in a 16th century double storeyed timber-framed building.

Clare

Another beautiful town, set on the river Stour, that is full of very old shops, and antique shops by the dozens. Many of the houses display pargetry work, which is ornamental plaster coating, a speciality of the region. Clare is a town to be walked around, and to enjoy the many historic buildings.

Early Closing Day: Wednesday.

Places to See

Castle & Priory remains. The Castle is dated before 1090. It has a Norman Motte and Bailey, and is surmounted by a circular stone Keep.

The Priory was built in 1248 on the site of the first house of the order of the Augustinian Friars. The prior's house, cellar and infirmary are still in use.

There is a timber-framed house in the village that dates from 1473, and once belonged to a priest.

The *Church of St Peter and St Paul* is mainly 15th century, but has an earlier tower. Inside the church there are some fine wood carvings, and there are also some on the chancel door.

The *Swan Inn* in the High Street has a wooden sign outside that is possibly the oldest in England. It is a solid carving 10 feet long. Believed to have originated from the castle, it shows the arms of England and France, probably commemorating the marriage of two ancient Clare families. Good home cooked meals are served in a pleasant, warm and cosy pub, and are reasonably priced.

The *Bell Inn* has been offering visitors warm hospitality since the 16th century.

The *Clare Hotel* is a very picturesque hotel that was once called the 'Rose & Crown'. It combines a traditional welcome with modern comforts. Good restaurant and the beer garden is delightful.

The *Cock Inn* is a traditional English pub offering good home cooked meals, and specialising in fresh fish dishes in the restaurant and the two bars or the beer garden. Early 17th century building combined with a converted barn make this a very interesting pub.

The *Globe*, originally a late 17th century L-shaped building, was re-fronted in white brick early in the 19th century. A very popular pub with locals, where visitors are made very welcome.

Chapel Cottage has an original 12th century doorway.

Country Walks: A 3½ miles circular walk starting at the Country Park is waymarked, allow 2 hours. The park has 30 acres on the river Stour.

Stoke-by-Clare

Fantastic little village spread out along the river on one of the most scenic drives in East Anglia. There was once a Benedictine priory, but its remains are now in the grounds of a private school. The Tudor dovecot near the church resembles a gatehouse.

Wine: *Boyton Vineyard*, Hill Farm, Boyton End. 2 acres of vineyard open early April to end of October 10.30am to 6pm. Admission charge includes tour, talk and wine tasting in its own wine lodge. The historic farmhouse is set in lovely gardens with a nice picnic area.

Turn right onto the A604.

Sturmer

A beautiful village with two manor houses, a church and lovely thatch and tile cottages.

The *Red Lion* is a pub that has been refurbished, and is so popular that at times there are not enough spaces in the car park. Very traditional pub with lots of charm and atmosphere.

> Turn right onto the B1061.

Kedington

The *Church of St Peter and St Paul* has an uneven brick floor, a three decker pulpit, a Saxon cross, a sermon timer rather like a large egg timer, fine carvings, and many interesting tombs. Open Easter to the end of September.

Behind the church is a row of ten elms each said to have a dead knight buried beneath. When one of the trees blew down, legend has it that a skeleton was found at its roots, but no ghosts have been seen.

The Barnardiston family, one of Suffolk's most important and oldest, stretches back 27 unbroken generations, and many of the family tombs are in the church.

The *Plough Inn*, ½ mile from Kedington towards Hundon, is not easy to find but is well worth the search, as the views from this recently and lovingly restored pub are magnificent. Meals are great and the servings are very generous at either the bar or in the restaurant.

> Turn left onto the A143.

Haverhill

Police: Swan Lane.
Places To See
Anne of Cleves House. Anne was the fourth wife of Henry VIII. He married her for purely political reasons in 1540 and divorced her a few months later. She was given a pension and spent the rest of her life in seclusion at Richmond Palace and at Haverhill.

The *Australian Arms* pub was supposedly given its name by a group of Irish railway workers who spoke about emigrating to Australia.
Golf: *Haverhill Golf Club Ltd*, Coupals Road. 9 holes parkland course with the river near three holes.

> Leave Haverhill on the A604, and take the first country road on the right.

Withersfield

A few little cottages, a church, and a nice pub called the *White Horse Inn* make up this small but very pretty village.

Great and Little Thurlow

The village of Great Thurlow comes alive on Boxing Day for the traditional Meet, and in September for the Thurlow Fayre. There are many 17th century cottages in Little Thurlow and the manor house is Georgian.

Great Thurlow has a restored mill.

Back onto the A143 pass through Wickham Street and Chedburgh on the way back to Bury St Edmunds.

TOUR 14

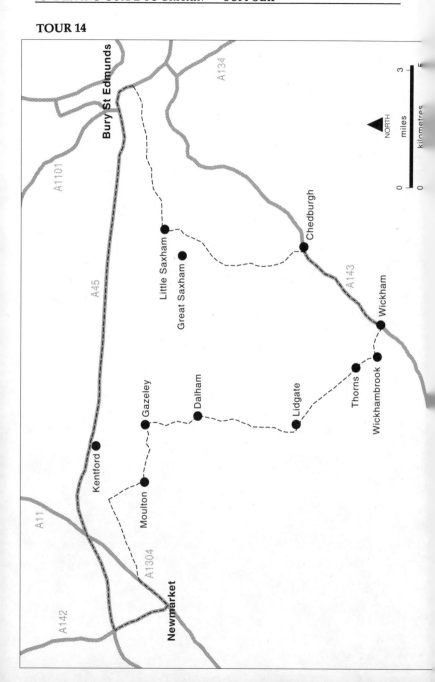

Tour 14 - Bury St Edmunds to Newmarket

Leave Bury on the A45, then turn left onto the B1506.

Kentford

At the crossroads between Newmarket and Bury is the grave of a gipsy boy, where punters lay flowers in the hope of bringing them good luck at the races.

Newmarket

Newmarket, on the A1304, has been the headquarters of British horse racing, breeding and training since 1605 when James I began hunting in the area. Spring and autumn races were held to coincide with his visits. Since Charles I, monarchs have continued their patronage and the town is surrounded by a heath where horses can still be seen exercising daily.

High Street is the ancient road between London and Norwich, and at one end is the Jubilee Clock tower, and at the other end is The Cooper Memorial Fountain.

Information Centre: 63 The Rookery, ph (01638) 667 200.

Hospital: Exning Road.

Police: Vicarage Road.

Places To See

The *Jockey Club*, built in 1772, is in the High Street.

A *cottage in Palace Street* is the only house left that was built before the great fire in 1683 which almost destroyed the town. It is reputed to have belonged to Nell Gwynne, mistress of Charles II.

The *Rutland Arms*, in High Street, dates back to Charles II.

National Stud, on the Heath two miles south-west of the town, ph (01638) 663 464, is open to the public April to November. Tours of the 500 acre farm are available and times are: weekdays 11.15am & 2.30pm, Saturday at 11.15am and Sunday at 2.30pm.

National Horseracing Museum and Newmarket Thoroughbred Tours, 99 High Street, ph (01638) 667 333. Open March to December from Tuesday to Saturday 10am to 5pm and Sunday 2 to 5pm, July and August Monday to Saturday from 10am to 5pm and Sunday 12noon to 5pm. Cameras are not allowed in the Museum. Many tours operate from the Museum, bookings are essential. No tours on Sunday or Monday, or from the end of October till March.

The Museum is packed with exhibits dating back to the origins of racing.

Golf: *Links Golf Club*, Cambridge Road, ph (01638) 663 000. 18 holes flat parkland course. No clubs for hire, a Handicap certificate is required and restrictions apply.

Leave Newmarket heading back to Bury on the B1506. Turn right through country roads.

Moulton

Nothing could be more beautiful than travelling through this fabulous countryside. There are farmland views all around the village and those coming down the hill into Moulton are a photographer's delight. This village, with its flint and thatch cottages surrounding the large village green, is definitely worth a visit. Why not drive slowly through the ford, which always has water in it? It's a great way to have your car washed.

Packhorse Bridge is narrow and so hump backed that all traffic now uses the by-road beside it. The River Kennett links Moulton to Dalham and Lidgate.

Gazeley

The *Church of All Saints* dates back to the 14th century. Annually on November 5, bells were rung to celebrate Guy Fawkes Day. At harvest time, the *gleaning* bell was rung to signify that gleaners could enter the fields. The *passing* bell was rung when someone died. The bells unfortunately no longer ring out over the countryside.

Dalham

Dalham has clusters of thatched cottages and a pond, and has to be one of the prettiest villages beside the river Kennett.

Dalham Hall belonged to the Rhodes family of which Cecil, of Africa fame, was a son. The Duke of Wellington also lived for some years at the Hall. Built in the early 1700s, it has lovely tree-lined avenues including one which leads directly to the church.

The village hall was erected to the memory of Cecil Rhodes by his brother Francis.

St Mary's Church has remarkable inscriptions and paintings which describe how the steeple was erected in 1625. Its spire was said to have fallen in a gale which swept England on the night that Cromwell died. Francis Rhodes was buried in the church in 1905.

The *Affleck Arms* is a thatched Elizabethan pub in the village centre, and guests can sit outside the front and view the river. The meals are excellent and very reasonably priced, and there is a play area and pets' corner for children.

Pass through Lidgate and Thorns and some of the most beautiful countryside in Suffolk.

Wickhambrook

This pretty little village has eleven greens with unusual names. There are three manor houses, flint cottages, a home bakery, and one and a half pubs - the *Plumbers Arms* has one very unique feature, half is in Wickhambrook the other half is in the village of Denston.

Turn left onto the A143 and pass through Wickham Street and Chedburgh. Turn left and pass through Chevington.

Great and Little Saxham

St Andrew's Church was restored in the 18th century and the interior has some very interesting features, including a Stuart pulpit, magnificent stained glass windows and a Perpendicular font. One of the brasses is to John Eldred dated 1632 who was the first person to bring nutmeg to Britain.

Saxham Hall was built by Hutchison Mure in 1779 and was added to in 1798 by the new owner, one Thomas Mills. The gardens were landscaped by *Capability Brown*.

The *Church of St Nicholas* in Little Saxham has a round Norman tower with a band of arches. There are two very interesting features. One is a monument to Thomas Fitzlucas which was altered in the 17th century to allow a monument to be built to William Crofts, who had entertained Charles II and Samuel Pepys. The other more famous item is the Stuart bier with sliding handles, which is very rare.

Return to Bury St Edmunds.

TOUR 15

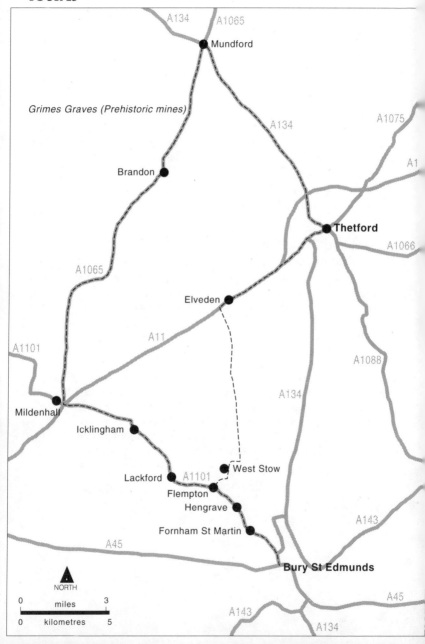

Tour 15 - Bury St Edmunds to Grimes Graves

Take the A1101 to the north-west.

Fornham St Martin

The village is centred around the *Church of St Martin*, and is one of the trio of villages of Fornham St Martin, Genevieve St Martin and Timworth St Martin.

The *Three King's* has bar meals, a carvery and an à la carte menu in the restaurant.

Golf: *Fornham Park Golf Club*, St John's Hill Plantation, ph (01284) 706 777. 18 holes of flat parkland with rivers and lakes, par 71. Visitors welcome, please phone in advance.

Hengrave

A picturesque, compact village on the river Lark, with cottages of thatch and flint. *Hengrave Hall* is a delightful Tudor mansion built in the mid 1500s. In the grounds is a lovely and fascinating little church with a round Saxon tower.

Flempton

Golf: *Flempton Park Golf Club*, ph (01284) 728 291. 9 holes of lovely, slightly undulating, well bunkered course. Restrictions apply.

Lackford

Nature Reserve: *Lackford Wildfowl Reserve*, off the A1101. Restored gravel pits where you can see wildfowl and waders.

Icklingham

The *Church of St James* in the centre of this little village was mentioned in the Domesday Book.

There are many tales of ghostly riders and legend has it that when riders on horseback came from Norwich and crossed the River Lark, even the quietest horse would take fright. A mound in the old roadway is said, even today, to make the quietest pony shy away and dogs and cats avoid the area at night.

The Normans introduced rabbits into the area and the rabbit has been mentioned in many folk stories. Often a white rabbit is seen at dusk walking along a path in the company of a witch. Sight of her has caused horses to bolt and men to die, and the well-worn path she uses to cross a track and pass into a field through a gap in the hedge that cannot be closed, covers the site of an early cemetery.

The *Plough Inn* will make you very welcome, and the staff will be only to pleased to enlighten you on the tales of the inn and the village.

After leaving the village, take the left hand fork, which is still the A1101.

Mildenhall

Police: Kingsway.
Places To See
Mildenhall & District Museum, King Street, is open February to Christmas on Wednesday, Thursday, Saturday & Sunday from 2.30 to 4.30pm. Friday only 11am to 4pm.

The museum has exhibits of local history, particularly of RAF Mildenhall, the Mildenhall Treasure, domestic and craft bygones, and natural history on the Fens and Breckland.

In 1946, over 30 pieces of 4th century Roman silverware were ploughed up in the area, but these are now displayed in the British Museum in London.

The *Church of St Mary* is built of Barnack stone with the North porch being the largest in Suffolk. Lodged in the angel roof of the nave are some arrowheads that were supposedly fired by Cromwell's supporters. Open Easter to October 11am to 3pm.

Wine: *Eros Vineyard*, Kenny Hill, ph (01375) 375 394. 16 acre vineyard open all year from 10am to 5pm. Entry is free, the vineyard has its own restaurant, woodland garden and picnic areas. In May and June there are tours of asparagus fields.

Travel north on the A1065.

Brandon

The town, built mainly of flint, lies in the north-west corner of the county, almost on the Norfolk border, on the banks of the Little Ouse river.

Market Days: Thursday & Saturday.
Places To See
Brandon Country Park was built in 1826 for Edward Bliss and the estate then consisted of about 2500 acres. The House has been restored and is now a privately owned hotel.

Thetford Forest Drive is open all year from 10am to 8pm or dusk if earlier. *Thetford High Lodge*, located in the heart of the forest, along Forest Drive, is the ideal place from which to explore Britain's largest lowland pine forest. The forest is home to four species of deer, rare red squirrel and the crossbill.

Brandon Heritage Centre, George Street, is open April to September on Thursday & Saturday from 10.30am to 5pm & Sunday 2pm to 5pm. October to mid-December on Thursday & Saturday from 10.30am to 4pm & Sunday 2pm to 4pm.

Here you can step back in time to the Stone Age by visiting a flintknappers' workshop and reliving the town's history.

The *Five Bells*, on Market Hill, has good bar meals, a lovely restaurant, and a nice patio outside.

Bicycle Hire: *High Lodge Forest Centre*, Thetford Forest Park, District Office, Santon Downham, ph (01842) 815 434.

Country Walks: *Santon Downham* offers a very pleasant two mile walk from the Forestry Commission Headquarters through the forest of beech, pine, poplar and willow trees. It joins the Thetford Road through a magnificent lime tree avenue.

Brandon Country Park, ph (01842) 810 185. 30 acres of landscaped parkland with a lake. Tree trail, forest walks and wayfaring course are open daily all year.

Boat Hire: *Bridge House Hotel*, Bridge Street, ph (01842) 813 137. Canoe/rowing boat hire on the Little Ouse River.

Continue on the A1065, then turn right onto a narrow dirt track lane, which leads up to the flint mines.

Grimes Graves

Grimes Graves is not, as its name suggests, a burial ground, but the site of 4000-year-old flint mines. The approach road is a narrow track leading to the grass covered hollows amongst pine and fir trees. One of the mine shafts is open for inspection, and is well worth the climb down the 30ft ladder to see how miners had to crawl on their hands and knees with picks made from antlers to chip out the flint for tools and weapons. There are over 300 worked pits covering about 35 acres and it is an amazing prehistoric site. The area surrounding the site is also steeped in history, and the remains of Weeting Castle and Weeting Heath are not far away.

Return to the A1065, then turn right, passing through Thetford Forest.

Mundford

The river Wissey meanders through the quiet beauty of the village. Cottages are mainly flint with thatched roofs, and there are some beautiful houses overlooking the village green. *Lynford Hall* has a huge estate, *West Hall* is a Tudor manor house, and along with *Rosemary Cottage* they are the oldest buildings in the village. *Pear Tree Inn*, now thatched cottages, is where drovers stayed and penned their stock at Nelson Cottage.

The *Church of St Leonard* built in the 13th century has a spire which is visible from all approaches to this lovely village.

Country Walks: There are many pleasant walks, all well sign posted, through the forest, where you will see squirrels, many beautiful birds and deer. The trees around the village are beech and the colours and the scent from them are wonderful.

Leave Munford on the A134.

Thetford

The rivers Thet and Little Ouse meet in the centre of this charming town, which was the capital for the Danes in the 9th century. In the 11th century there were 13 churches in the town.

Thomas Paine, the author of the *Rights of Man* and the *Age of Reason*, was born in White Hart Street in 1737. He migrated to America and died in New York in 1809. A statue of him stands outside the Bell Hotel.

Police: Norwich Road.

Places To See

Ancient House Museum, White Hart Street, is in a 15th century building, and has exhibits of local history.

Castle Hill Earthworks, Castle Lane, are all that remain of the castle which was demolished in 1173.

Priory Ruins, Water Lane, are the remains of the Cluniac Priory of Our Lady, founded in 1103.

Charles Burrell Museum, Minstergate, ph (01842) 751 166. Open April to October, Saturday, Sunday and Bank Holidays 10am to 5pm. Admission charge. Suitable for wheelchair access.

The Museum draws together an impressive collection of exhibits to tell the story of Charles Burrell & Son, a name once famous throughout the world. The large display of steam traction engines are housed on the ground floor, together with a series of re-created workshops with original tools and machinery. Up in the gallery a series of photographs, letters and documents illustrate both the Company and the Family.

The 16th century *Bell Hotel* is a mainly Elizabethan half-timbered building overlooking the river and a three way bridge.

The flint and brick *Dolphin Inn* is dated 1694.

Golf: *Thetford Golf Club*, Brandon Road, ph (01842) 752 169. 18 holes championship heathland course. Restrictions apply.

Town Trails: There is a two hour walk around this Breckland town dating back to Saxon times. A variety of buildings, old and new, can be seen including the Ancient House Museum, where many of the exhibits relate to features seen on the walk.

Leave Thetford on the A11 heading south.

Elveden

Elveden Hall is set in parklands, lakes and forests, and was built by the Maharaja Duleep Singh in 1888. The building has carved marble, eastern architecture and a dome of beaten copper.

The estate houses and alms-houses are of red brick, and Chalk Farm is the oldest house in the village. It has plastered mud and straw walls and is flint faced.

The *Church of St Andrew and St Patrick* dates from the 12th century.

Leave the village and take the next turn left onto the B1106 then turn right.

West Stow

West Stow Country Park & Anglo Saxon Village is open every day, and admission is free. Hours in winter are from 8am to 5pm; in summer from 8am to 8pm.

The Park is home to 120 species of birds, and over 20 species of animals have been sighted in the 125 acres of heathland, woodland and large lake bordered by the River Lark. There is a nature trail linking the heathland with the woods, river and lake.

The Anglo Saxon Village has pigs, hens and growing crops, and shows what farming was like in those days. Sometimes you can see and talk to *Anglo-Saxons* when the houses are occupied by people in costume. Craft courses and demonstrations are regularly provided.

On the same road as the Country Park and Anglo-Saxon Village is *CowWise* where you can watch the Friesian and Jersey cows being milked, and see calves and milking goats. There are plenty of young animals to feed including lambs and kids.

Nature Reserves: *West Stow Country Park* is a heathland nature reserve with woodland, river and lake.

Return to Bury St Edmunds on the A1101.

Tour 16 - Bury St Edmunds to Scole

Take the A45 to Ipswich then turn left about 13 miles from Bury. The road is well signposted to Haughley.

Haughley

Quaint village complete with moat, ducks and some pretty thatched cottages.

Haughley Park is open May to September on Tuesday only, 3 to 5.30pm. Admission charge, and suitable for wheelchair access. It is a Jacobean manor house with lovely gardens and woods set in parkland.

The *King's Arms*, a warm cream-painted pub dating from the 1500s, has heavily beamed ceilings and dark furniture. The food is excellent, from the traditional to the exotic.

Just before Wetherden turn right.

Wetherden

The flint *Church of St Mary* stands in a tree-encircled churchyard and has a beautiful hammerbeam roof.

Haughley Green

The town has a lovely church with a thatched roof.

Turn left.

Earl's Green

Between Haughley Green and Earl's Green are some delightful cottages and farms, and beautiful scenery. The drive is certainly worth taking.

Pass through Wyverstone Street then turn right.

Wyverstone

Leafy lanes, green fields, wide grass verges, a lovely church with a massive tower, and thatched cottages make this a definite must-see.

TOUR 16

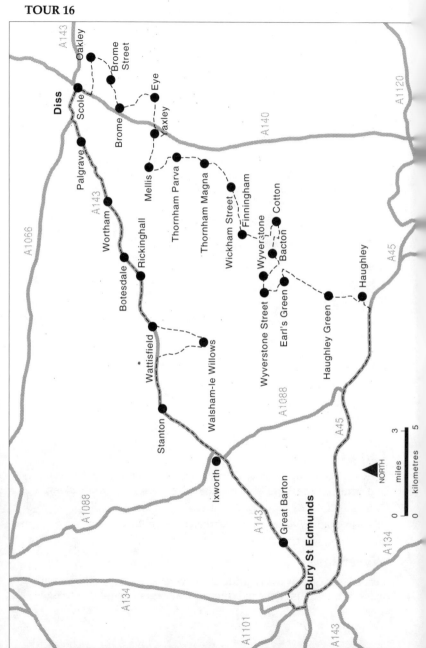

Bacton

Beautiful little village based around seven greens. Perpendicular *St Mary's Church* dates from the 14th and 15th centuries.

The *Bull* pub in the village serves a good traditional Sunday lunch, good bar meals, and has full à la carte menu. Children are well catered for and have an enclosed play area.

Cross the B1113.

Cotton

Mechanical Music Museum is open June to September on Sunday 2.30pm to 5.30pm. It has an extensive collection that includes organs, street pianos, polyphones, gramophones, musical boxes, musical dolls and a Wurlitzer Theatre pipe organ in a specially re-constructed cinema.

The large flint *Church of St Andrew* is 14th century.

The *Trowel & Hammer* is a most beautiful 14th century thatched pub and has been twice named *Pub of the Year*. The oak beamed restaurant is tastefully decorated, and the food is excellent, with fresh local produce and Greek cuisine specialties. Bar meals and ploughman's lunches are very good and reasonably priced. In the summer, lunch is served outside by the inground pool, where you are welcome to take a dip.

Drive back to the B1113, then turn right.

Finningham

Very pleasant drive through here as there are lots of lovely farm houses, thatched cottages and old churches.

The *White Horse* is a 15th century coaching inn with old timbers, pictures, brasses and cottage furniture. Have a meal in the cosy bar or in the restaurant. Home-made soup and steak & kidney pies are excellent and are reasonably priced.

Turn right and pass through Wickham Street.

Thornham Magna

The *Four Horseshoes* is a most delightful thatched, white painted pub dating from 1150. The interior is as good as the exterior, with low exposed beams, uneven floor, dark furniture and a beautiful long panelled bar. The meals are superb with generous servings and are reasonably priced. The accommodation is excellent, all rooms have ensuites, and some have sloping ceilings.

Thornham Parva

Thornham Parva's tiny thatched church has a 14th century octagonal font, a medieval painting and is a must-see.
Country Walks: *Thornham Walks and Field Centre*, Redhouse Yard, ph (01379) 788 153. Open 9am to 6pm daily. Closed some weekends from October to March. Herb Garden & Nursery and 12 miles of walks alongside 2000 acres of farmland with surfaced walkways to allow pushchair and wheelchair access.

Turn left.

Mellis

Pleasant and friendly, unspoilt little village with a great expanse of grass and wonderful wildlife. *St Mary's Church* has a tomb from the 16th century belonging to Francis Yaxley, a diplomat, who was sent to the Tower of London for betraying secrets.

Turn right in the village for Yaxley.

Yaxley

Yaxley Manor appears in records in 1066. Bull's Hall, another of the fine local manor houses, was transferred to William Bull in 1328 from Edward III, and is now privately owned.

Cross the A140 at the crossroads then turn right.

Eye

A fascinating town with character. Beautiful old houses, antique and interesting shops make up this lovely 18th century market town.
Police: Victoria Road.
Early Closing Day: Tuesday.
Places To See
The remains of a *Norman Castle* dated from 1156 are worth seeing, and there are great views of the town and the surrounding countryside from the top of the remains.
The Pennings is a lovely picnic spot and wildlife area.
Linden House, in Lambeth Street, is dated 1750.
The Guildhall dates from 1470 and stands between the church and the

primary school, once the grammar school.

The *Church of St Peter and St Paul* was founded in the 12th century, and has a rood screen dating from 1470 and a magnificent 100ft tower which dominates the landscape. Open daily 7.15am to 6.30pm.

Golf: *Diss Golf Club*, Stuston, ph (01379) 622 847. 18 holes and restrictions apply.

Take the north road leading to Diss then turn right.

Brome

This is a cute little village, certainly worth the drive. The First Marquis of Cornwallis built *Brome Hall* in 1590, and the Cornwallis family lived in the house until the early 1800s. A new house was built in 1960.

The Marquis was a general in the Revolutionary War and helped capture New York in 1776. He was also Governor-General and Commander in Chief of India from 1786 to 1793 and again in 1805, and served as Viceroy and Commander in Chief of Ireland from 1798 to 1801.

The *Church of St Mary* has stood for over one thousand years on its present site, and contains memorials to the Cornwallis family. The church is considered to be an outstanding example of restoration work by Thomas Jekyll. It also has the largest collection of sculptures by the well known Suffolk sculptor James Williams. The distinguished portrait painter Henry Walton is buried in the churchyard.

Oaksmere is a beautiful house that was once the original rectory, and it is set in spacious grounds with a Yew tree hedge, known as the *Dancing Ladies*. Opposite is the Old Curacy, is a thatched house of great character dating back to 1540.

Pass through Brome Street .

Oakley

The *Church of St Nicholas*, like its counterpart in Brome, has stood on the present site for over one thousand years.

Turn left onto the A143.

Scole

The *White Hart* is a lovely red brick, three-storey, Dutch gabled pub built at the crossroads in 1655.

St Andrew's Church was deliberately set on fire in 1963, destroying the entire roof. Almost facing the south porch is a unique headstone commemorating the re-interment of four Christians who were originally buried in the village some 1600 years before.

Leave Scole on the A143 and pass through Palgrave.

Wortham

The *Olde Tea Shoppe* is a converted Elizabethan haybarn adjoining the Post Office Store in the village. Morning coffee, teas, snacks and meals are served daily from 9am to 6pm in winter and 9am to 8pm in summer. It features lovely home cooking, and beautiful old timber settles and chairs. There is ample parking and children are more than welcome. There are also great gifts and handcrafts for sale.

Botesdale

Crown Hill House, at the top of the hill, was once a coaching inn and has an upper storey that still juts out over the pavement.

Rickinghall

The two villages known as Superior and Inferior follow an underground stream which runs through them, and passes right through *Hamlyn House*, originally a mill in the 17th century, now a fascinating pub. Lovely timber-framed buildings, some with thatch, line the village street.

There are two churches, both named St Mary's. The Upper church has been closed for many years but is well worth a visit. The Lower church, with its round tower, dates from the 13th century.

Pass through Wattisfield then turn left.

Walsham Le Willows

The village is set amongst beautiful trees, including lime, beech and, of course, willows.

Walsham Village Museum, in St Mary's Church, has changing exhibitions on local history.

The *Six Bells Inn* is 16th century and gets its name from the church tower. Serves good bar meals, has a nice garden and ample parking.

The church has a fascinating history, and pews of unmarried girls who have died are marked with a medallion.

Drive back onto the A143 then turn left.

Stanton

Stanton was mentioned in the Domesday Book, but the Romans were there before that. There are some very attractive 16th century houses in the village.

Stanton has two medieval churches, *All Saints* and *St John the Baptist*. Although St John's is roofless, the villagers still hold a service there once a year.

Wine: *Wyken Hall Gardens & Wyken Vineyards*, Stanton, ph (01359) 250 287. 7 acres of vines and 4 acres of garden open 1 February to 24 December, Thursday, Friday, Sunday and Bank Holiday Mondays 10am to 4pm. Closed during Easter week. Visit the gardens, country shop and cafe, Elizabethan Manor House and 16th century barn.

Country Walks: *Wyken Hall* has a spectacular woodland walk.

Continue on to Ixworth.

Ixworth

There are many lovely 14th century timber-framed houses in the village. The Church of St Mary dates back to the 14th century but has later additions.

Ixworth Abbey. The Blount family founded a Priory in the 12th century for St Augustine. The remains and an interesting crypt lie on the river Blackbourne, hidden among trees.

Nature Trail & Bird Reserve: *Ixworth Thorpe Farm*. The Manor farm on the A1088 is open on special days and other times by appointment, ph (01359) 269 444 or (01359) 269 386 evenings.

Wetland Bird Reserve has a 2 mile nature trail and 2 hides.

Great Barton

Great Barton started as a Saxon settlement and by the 13th century had become the *granary* for Bury St Edmunds.

Return to Bury St Edmunds.

TOUR 17

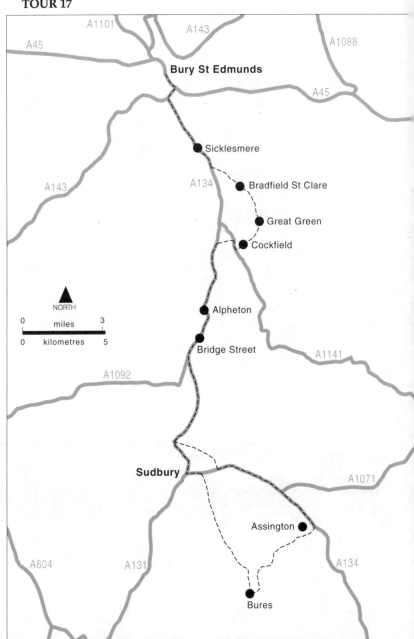

Tour 17 - Bury St Edmunds to Sudbury and Country Trail

Leave Bury St Edmunds on the A134 heading for Sudbury. Turn left and pass through Little Welnetham, then turn right. The countryside around here is very picturesque, and driving along these country roads is well worthwhile.

Bradfield St Clare

Bradfield St Clare, Bradfield Combust and Cockfield make up a delightful trio of villages. St Clare Hall is a 13th century moated manor.

Bradfield Woods once belonged to the Abbey and are well known for rare flora and fauna, particularly nightingales.

Pass through Great Green.

Cockfield

This is the largest village in Suffolk, and boasts *nine greens*. Some of the delightful little thatched cottages have very tiny windows and thick walls.

Bulls Wood is an ancient coppiced woodland.

Turn right, then left onto the A134 to Alpheton.

Alpheton

Although the A134 now divides this little village, it has been a settlement since 991AD. Two oak trees were planted in 1887 and the village pump was installed to commemorate the Jubilee of Queen Victoria.

The village's claim to fame was as the location for the film *Twelve O'Clock High* which starred Gregory Peck.

Pass through Bridge Street.

Sudbury

Sudbury is located on the A134 and was once the largest of East Anglia's woollen centres. Weaving is still carried on here.

Information Centre: Town Hall, Market Hill, ph (01787) 881 320 .
Hospital: West Suffolk Hospital, Hardwick Lane, Bury St Edmunds.
Police: Acton Lane.
Market Days: Thursday and Saturday.
Early Closing Day: Wednesday.
Places To See
Gainsborough's House, Market Hill, is open Easter to October from Tuesday to Saturday 10am to 5pm & Sunday 2 to 5pm. November to Easter, Tuesday to Saturday 10am to 4pm & Sunday 2 to 4pm. Closed Monday, Good Friday and between Christmas & New Year.

The house has a Georgian facade and was built in 1727 by his father, before the famous artist was born.
Quay Theatre is in restored Maltings (malt-houses) on the River Stour, and provides a regular program of drama, films and music.
Corn Exchange, Market Hill, built in 1841 is now the Public Library.
Market Hill is the centre of the town and in the square is a bronze statue of Thomas Gainsborough. The Town Hall built in 1828, still houses the Mayor's Parlour.
Salters Hall, now a Public School, is a 15th century timber-framed building with fine oriel windows.
All Saint's Church, built in the 15th century, has a carved tracery pulpit.
St Peter's Church is 15th century, and has painted screen panels and a 15th century embroidery done on velvet. Although no longer in use, the church is run by the Friends of St Peter's. Classical concerts are held here from time to time.
St Gregory's on the Croft is a lovely 14th century church and has one of the finest medieval font covers in the country.
Golf: *Newton Green Golf Club*, Newton Green. 9 holes flat common land course. Restrictions apply.
Horse Riding: *High Banks* on Melford Road.
Twinstead Riding Centre and Riding School, Twinstead.
Fishing: Excellent coarse fishing in the waters of the River Stour. A day licence is available from local tackle shops.
Boat Hire: Rowing boats can be hired in the summer from the Boathouse, Ballingdon Bridge.
Cruises: Take a steam launch trip on the River Stour, and see some of the beautiful country that inspired Thomas Gainsborough.
Tours: *Talbot Tours*, ph (01787) 374 745. Vintage coach tours around Sudbury, visiting silk weaving, traditional brickworks and the Quay Theatre. Tours available from May to September.

Leave Sudbury on the B1508.

Bures

Very pretty little village nestled in the valley of the Stour river on the edge of Constable Country. The village is divided as it lies in the two counties of Suffolk and Essex. Bures St Mary in Suffolk has the church and most of the village, while Bures Hamlet has the rail link to Sudbury and London.

Edmund was crowned King here at the age of 15 on Christmas Day 855AD. The Chapel was consecrated in 1218 and is half a mile out of the village on the road to Boxford.

Leave this very pretty village, take the country lanes to Assington then turn left onto the A134 and return to Bury St Edmunds. OR continue through the village and again along country lanes to join the A134. Turn left, bypass Sudbury and Long Melford and return to Bury.

ACCOMMODATION
Self Catering

Badwell Ash - Tour 12
Lodge Cottage
Badwell Ash Hall
Badwell Ash Bury St Edmunds
IP31 3JG
ph: (01359) 259 643
Contact: Mrs M Castro
1 cottage, sleeps 8
Weekly rate: £250.00-415.00, open
all year

Luxuriously appointed beamed
country cottage with central
heating, log fires, 2 bathrooms and
linen supplied. Games room and
conservatory with indoor barbecue.
Children are welcome and there is a
½ acre of private garden.

Brent Eleigh - Tour 2
Corrie Cottage
Hill Farm (Suffolk) Ltd
Brent Eleigh Sudbury 1C10 9PB
ph: (01787) 247 296
Contact: Mr J Sainsbury
1 Cottage, sleeps 7 + cot, open all
year
Weekly rate: £140.00-330.00

Beautiful thatched cottage with
large sheltered gardens set in the
most fantastic countryside where
the scenery is unbelievable.
Children are welcome in this
historic house and there are
beautiful gardens to play in. Linen
is provided and gas/electricity is

by meter. An absolute must for
those wishing to tour around the
historic town of Lavenham and
many historic places of interest.

Copdock - Tour 1
Hall Farm Cottage
Hall Farm
Church Lane
Copdock Ipswich IP8 3JZ
ph: (01473) 730 287
Contact: Mrs Carr
1 cottage, sleeps 4, open
April- September
Weekly rate: £200.00-300.00

The centrally heated cottage is
part of a period farmhouse with
an open fireplace, and children
are welcome. Close to Constable
Country and many historic places
of interest this quiet, comfortable
and well equipped cottage is an
ideal touring base.

Cransford - Tour 9
Wood Lodge
High House Farm
Cransford Woodbridge IP13
9PD
ph: (01728) 663 461
Contact: Mrs Sarah Kindred
1 house, sleeps 6-8, open all year
Weekly rate: £175.00-400.00

Beautiful country retreat, spacious
gamekeeper's lodge in ½ acre garden

set in 18 acres of woodland. Children are welcome in this well equipped house where linen is provided and gas/electricity are by meter.

Dunwich - Tour 9

Cliff House
Minsmere Road
Dunwich IP17 3DQ
ph: (01728) 648 282
Contact: Alan or Penny Harris
2 cottages, 3 bungalows, 8 flats, sleep 2-7
Weekly rate: £65.00-150.00

Country house set in 30 acres of woodland with beach, adjoining Dunwich Heath (National Trust) and Minsmere Nature Reserve & Bird Sanctuary. Children are welcome, there is a play area and games room. Fishing, golf, many nature trails and country walks are all available from well equipped accommodation.

Hitcham - Tour 11

Old Wetherden Hall Cottage
Old Wetherden Hall
Hitcham Ipswich IP7 7PZ
ph: (01449) 740574
Contact: Mrs J Elsden
1 house, sleeps 6, open all year
Weekly rate: £120.00-300.00

15th century moated hall with oak beams, set in a beautiful secluded large garden. Children are welcome in this centrally heated self-contained, well-equipped unit with linen provided. Horse riding, fishing and an abundance of wildlife make this an ideal touring base.

Playford - Tour 3

The Olde Post Office
Glenham
Hill Farm Road
Playford Ipswich IP6 9DU
ph: (01473) 624 939
Contact: Mr & Mrs GC Booker
1 cottage, sleeps 5, open all year
Weekly rate: £70.00-180.00

Delightful cottage in beautiful peaceful country setting, where children are more than welcome. The gardens are lovely and there is ample car parking. The cottage is well equipped, pleasantly furnished and has an enchanting curved spiral staircase up to traditional rooms with low ceilings and latched doors. Electricity is by meter and linen is provided to overseas guests. B&B is also available in the main house, where the atmosphere is very homely, breakfasts are great and the furnishings delightful. This is certainly a fantastic place to be based for touring and where Jose & Geoff will make you part of the family.

Bed & Breakfast

Belchamp St Paul - Tour 17

The Cherry Tree Inn
Knowl Green
Belchamp St Paul Sudbury CO10 7BY
ph: (01787) 237 263
Contact: Mr & Mrs Oliver
1 double, 1 twin, both with private facilities
Double B&B: £30.00

Thatched pub set in beautiful countryside with lovely views and excellent, inexpensive meals. Children are welcome and there is a games room and outdoor equipment in the gardens. Ideal base for touring East Anglia. Golf, fishing, horse riding are all available nearby.

Bures - Tour 17

Butlers
Colne Road
Bures Hamlet Bures CO8 5DN
ph: (01787) 227 243
3 double, 2 twin, ensuites 2, private 1
Single B&B: from £19.00

Beautifully restored 17th century beamed farmhouse set in quiet and peaceful countryside, in a picturesque village with delightful views. Ideal for walking, and shooting is allowed on the property. 18 hole golf course nearby at Nayland and horse riding is also available nearby.

Bury St Edmunds - Tour 12

Dunston Guest House Hotel
8 Springfield Road
Bury St Edmunds IP33 3AN
ph: (01284) 767 981
6 single, 7 double, 3 twin, 7 family, ensuites 8, private 4 Single B&B: £20-£27.50, Double B&B: £36-£40.00

Lovely Victorian house, providing first class accommodation, situated in a quiet tree-lined street 10 minutes walk from town centre. All rooms have TV, telephones and tea/coffee making facilities. Car parking facilities and a lovely garden make this an ideal place to stop in Bury. Children are welcome and there is wheelchair accessibility.

Cransford - Tour 9

High House Farm
Cransford Framlingham IP13 9PD
ph: (01728) 663 461
Contact: Mrs Sarah Kindred
1 double with ensuite, 1 family with private facilities
Single B&B: £24.00, Double B&B: £36.00

Beautifully restored 15th century farmhouse with exposed beams, inglenooks and lovely gardens. Children are welcome at half price. Rooms have TV, tea/coffee making facilities. Ideally located between Framlingham and Saxmundham for touring or visiting places of interest. Fishing, golf and horse riding are all nearby.

Dunwich - Tour 9

The Ship Inn
St James Street
Dunwich IP17 3DU
Contact: Ann Marshlain
Single B&B: £20.00

In the heart of the village this beautiful old inn dates back to Tudor times, but has Georgian and Victorian additions. The atmosphere in the pub is one where everyone is made welcome. Double rooms, one has ensuite, are attractive with frilly duvets and leaded windows. The same menu serves both restaurant and the mellow bar hung with fishing nets and floats. Regulars come in for a pint of the local brew, Adnams of Southwold, and to eat the expertly cooked fresh fish that has travelled all of 20 yards from boat to table.

Earl Soham - Tour 3

The Falcon
Earl Soham Framlingham
ph: (01728) 685 263
Contact: Paul & Lavina Algar
1 single, 1 double, 2 twin, all with ensuites
Single B&B: from £19.00, Double: £38.00

Delightful 15th century half timber-framed non-smoking hotel with open log fires and cosy bars where a great welcome awaits. The very pretty village is set in wonderful countryside and offers lovely walks and bird watching. The reasonably priced meals are excellent and served in either the bar or the restaurant. Children are very welcome to stay and to dine in the restaurant.

Fressingfield - Tour 10

Chippenham Hall
Fressingfield Eye IP21 5TD
ph: (01379) 586 733
Contact: Mrs Sargent
3 doubles with ensuites
Daily rate: From £54.00-60.00 per room

Tudor manor house set in 7 acres of delightfully secluded gardens in rural area. This friendly, heavily beamed hall with its inglenook fireplace is a great place to relax or to visit the many places of interest. Children over 12 are welcome and special rates apply in winter. Golf and horse riding are available nearby and the indoor pool is available for guests' use.

Hacheston - Tour 9

Cherry Tree House
The Street
Hacheston Woodbridge IP13 0DR
ph: (01728) 746 371
2 single, 1 double, 1 twin, ensuites 2, private 2
Single B&B: £16.00

17th century farm house with

lovely garden which guests and children are welcome to use. Horse riding, fishing and golf are all available nearby.

Hadleigh - Tour 2

Odds and Ends
131 High Street
Hadleigh IP7 5EG
ph: (01473) 822 032
Contact: Ann Stephenson
2 double, 4 twin, ensuites 5
Single B&B: £19.00, Double/Twin B&B: £35.00

Traditional 16th century house with Georgian appearance offers lovely comfortable accommodation within easy walking distance of shops and restaurants. Ground floor rooms with wheelchair access are available. Children and dogs are welcome in this charming, centrally heated house where special rates apply to winter breaks. Golf is available nearby and town trails around this historic town are a must.

Hartest - Tour 13

Gifford's Hall
Hartest Bury St Edmunds IP29 4EX
ph: (01284) 830 464
Contact: John Kemp
1 double, 2 twin, all with ensuites
Single B&B: £22.00, Double B&B: £34.00-38.00

Lovely historic Georgian farmhouse with 33 acres of vineyards, wild flower meadows, rose gardens and animals. The lovely large rooms have tea/coffee making facilities, TV, radios and telephones, with attractive views over peaceful countryside. This is a non-smoking establishment. Children and pets are welcome in this centrally heated house which has a games room, restaurant and is licensed.

Hintlesham - Tour 2

College Farm
Hintlesham Ipswich IP8 3NT
ph: (01473) 652 253
Contact: Mrs Rosemary Bryce
1 single, 1 double with ensuite, 1 twin /family
Single B&B: £16.00-25.00, Double/Twin B&B: from £36.00

Children over 5 are welcome at this beamed 15th century farmhouse set in a beautiful quiet rural setting on a 100 acre arable/beef farm. Tea/coffee making facilities in rooms, separate guest TV lounge with log fire, lovely gardens, ample car parking facilities, and tennis court and horse riding/pony trekking nearby. This delightful home is situated between Ipswich and Hadleigh close to historic Lavenham and Constable Country.

Kessingland - Tour 5

The Old Rectory
157 Church Road
Kessingland NR33 7SQ
ph: (01502) 740 020
2 double, 1 twin, all with ensuites
Single B&B: £24.00, Double B&B: £44.00

Beautiful late-Georgian house set

back from the road in 2 acres of lovely gardens. Children and guests are made very welcome in this comfortable home furnished with antiques. Golf, horse riding and fishing are all available nearby.

Lavenham - Tour 2

Angel Hotel
Market Place
Lavenham C010 9QZ
ph: (01787) 247 388
Contact: Roy & Anne Whitworth and John Barry
6 double, 1 twin, 1 family, all with ensuites
Single B&B: £40.00-50.00, Double B&B: £50.00-70.00

Historic inn, built in 1420, where children are welcome. The bars are have a very cosy atmosphere with scrubbed pine and dark oak furniture, bookshelves, china and paintings. All rooms have ensuites, TV and telephones. Meals are reasonably priced and can be served at the bar, in the restaurant or outside on the market place frontage. There is a garden and courtyard at the rear of the pub. 18 hole golf course at Newton Green and horse riding nearby.

Long Melford - Tour 13

The George & Dragon
Long Melford
ph: (01787) 371 285
Contact: Peter, Marilyn or Ian Thorogood
2 double, 3 twin, 1 family all with ensuites

Single B&B: £30.00, Double/family: £50.00

In the centre of the village, this real 16th century village inn has been lovingly restored. The bar meals are home-made from local produce and are very reasonably priced. Children and dogs are welcome and there is wheelchair accessibility on the ground floor. All rooms have tea/coffee making facilities, TV and telephones. This really is a great place to stay while exploring Suffolk and a stroll around this wonderful village is certainly a must. Special rates apply for winter breaks.

Mendlesham Green - Tour 6

Cherry Tree Farm
Mendlesham Green Stowmarket
IP14 5RQ
ph: (01449) 766 376
Contact: Mr & Mrs Ridsdale
2 double with en-suites, 1 double with private facilities
Double B&B: from £40.00

Lovely farm house set in a quiet picturesque village. This charming friendly home has a guest lounge with a log fire which is very welcome after touring on colder days. Evening meals are available, home-made bread, garden fresh vegetables, and East Anglian wine to complement a lovely meal.

Orford - Tour 3

Crown & Castle Hotel
Orford IP12 2LJ

ph: (01394) 450 205
2 single, 5 double, 12 twin, 1 family, ensuites 16, private 1
B&B: from £32.50-65.00 per room

Old timber coaching inn, opposite the castle. Very friendly and relaxed atmosphere in this privately owned hotel where children are welcome. Four poster beds grace some of the rooms which are tastefully furnished. Special rates apply for short breaks. Fishing, golf, horse riding, and boating are all available nearby.

Playford - Tour 3
Glenham
Hill Farm Road
Playford Ipswich IP6 9DU
ph: (01473) 624 939
Contact: Mrs & Mrs GC Booker
1 single, 1 double, 1 twin
Single B&B: from £15.00

Situated in the beautiful Fynn Valley just north of Ipswich, this delightful B&B is a home away from home. The friendliness here is second to none and Jose & Geoff will make you feel part of the family. Breakfasts are huge and well presented in the beautiful dining room and are certainly a great way to start the day. Ideal touring base, where children are welcome, for visiting the many places of interest. There is a cottage attached to the main house with an enchanting curved spiral staircase leading to traditionally furnished low ceiling bedrooms. Golf, horse riding, nature trails and the coast are all nearby.

Shelly - Tour 2
Sparrows
Shelly Hadleigh 1P7 5RQ
ph: (01206) 337 381
Contact: Mrs Rachel Thomas
2 double (1 double can be family), with ensuites
Single B&B: £18.00, Double B&B: £34.00

Children are welcome in this 15th century farmhouse in beautiful countryside where excellent walking, fishing, tennis, table tennis and bicycles are available. 3 local pubs with high standard food just 2 miles away make this an ideal touring base. Rooms have TV, radios, telephones and tea/coffee making facilities.

Stoke-by-Nayland - Tour 8
Thorington Hall
Stoke-by-Nayland CO6 4SS
ph: (01206) 337 329
Contact: Mrs Deirdre Wollaston
2 single, 2 double, all with private facilities
Single B&B: £15.00-17.50, Double B&B: £40.00-47.00

Beautiful 17th century National Trust House set in the heart of Constable Country, between Stoke-by-Nayland and Higham on the edge of the tiny hamlet of Thorington Street. Children and dogs are welcome, and special rates apply for 3 or more days and for children under 12 years. Fishing, golf, horse riding, nature trails and sailing are all available nearby.

Thorington Street - Tour 8

Nether Hall
Thorington Street
Stoke-by-Nayland CO6 4ST
ph: (01206) 337 373
Contact: Mr & Mrs Jackson
1 single, 2 double. all with ensuites
Single B&B: £21.00, Double B&B: £42.00

Charming 15th century Country House with walled garden and meadows adjoining the River Box, in the unspoilt heart of Constable Country. Children are welcome in this beautiful home with lovely rooms equipped for disabled guests with TV, radio, telephone and tea/coffee making facilities. Fishing, golf and horse riding are available nearby.

Thornham Magna - Tour 16

The Four Horseshoes
Wickham Road
Thornham Magna IP23 8HD
ph: (01379) 678 777
2 single, 6 double, 2 twin, 1 family, ensuites 10
Single room: £35.00, Double room: £55.00

Beautiful thatched, large open plan pub dating back to 1150. Exposed beams, dark furniture, long panelled bar and crazy floors make this one of the most charming pubs in Suffolk. Centrally heated ensuite bedrooms have private telephones as well as TV, hospitality tray, and the country views from the little windows are magnificent. Room 21 is a family room built around a Tudor chimney where the roof curves and slants above matched pine furniture.

Thurston - Tour 11

The Grange Hotel
Thurston Bury St Edmunds IP31 1PQ
2 single, 2 twin, 8 double, 2 family, ensuites 12, private 3
Single B&B: from £35.00, Double/Twin B&B: from £50.00

Country House Hotel with resident Chef-Proprietor whose bar meals and a la carte menu are a delight 7 days a week. The terrace and garden are delightful. There is accessibility for disabled guests, and children and dogs are welcome. All rooms have TV, telephones and tea/coffee making facilities. Special rates apply for short breaks.

Woodbridge - Tour 3

Seckford Hall
Woodbridge IP13 6NU
ph: (01394) 385 678
3 single, 6 double, 5 twin, 18 family, all with ensuites
Single B&B: £79.00, Double B&B: £99.00

This delightful 16th century romantic Elizabethan country house hotel is set in 34 acres of gardens and woodlands in picturesque countryside. All rooms have four poster beds, ensuites, telephone and many other facilities, and there is a restaurant, indoor heated swimming pool and gym. An 18 hole golf course, shooting on the property and fishing make this a very pleasant way to relax and enjoy the good life. Horse riding is available nearby. Children are welcome and are at reduced rates at certain times of the year. Special rates apply for short breaks. Ideal base for exploring many places of interest.

Worlington - Tour 12

Brambles
Mildenhall Road
Worlington   Bury St Edmunds
IP28 8RY
ph: (01638) 713 121
2 twin, 2 single, all with ensuites
Single B&B: £20.00, Double B&B: £50.00

Beautiful country house set in 3 acres of garden on the edge of the village next to the golf club. Children are welcome in this large and spacious home furnished with antiques.

INDEX OF SIGHTS AND ATTRACTIONS

Covehithe	St Andrew's	Tour 5
Lindsey	St James Chapel	Tour 2
Long Melford	Holy Trinity	Tour 13
Thornham	Parva	Tour 16

Constable Country

East Bergholt, Dedham, Flatford, Stratford St Mary	Tour 8

Craft Centres

Aldringham	Craft Market	Tour 3
Blythburgh	Blythburgh Pottery	Tour 9
Butley	Butley Pottery	Tour 3
Debenham	Carter's Kiln & Pottery	Tour 6
Dedham	Dedham Art & Crafts	Tour 8
Earl Stonham	Ascot House Crafts	Tour 6
Horringer	Horringer Crafts	Tour 12
Kersey	Kersey Pottery	Tour 2
Monks Eleigh	Corn craft	Tour 2
Needham Market	The Old Piggery Pottery	Tour 6
Stonham Aspal	Craft centre	Tour 6
Wilby	Wilby Pottery	Tour 6
Wrentham	Willow basketry	Tour 5

Early Closing Days

Beccles	Wednesday	Tour 5
Bury St Edmunds	Thursday	Tour 12
Clare	Wednesday	Tour 13
Dedham	Wednesday	Tour 8
Eye	Tuesday	Tour 16
Framlingham	Wednesday	Tour 4
Hadleigh	Wednesday	Tour 2
Ipswich	Wednesday	Tour 1
Lowestoft	Thursday	Tour 5
Needham Market	Tuesday	Tour 6
Orford	Wednesday	Tour 3
Somerleyton	Tuesday	Tour 5
Stowmarket	Tuesday	Tour 11
Sudbury	Wednesday	Tour 17

Farm Parks

Cavendish	Pentlow Farm	Tour 13
Dedham	Rare Breed Farm	Tour 8
Earsham	Home of the Otter	Tour 10
Easton	Farm Park	Tour 4
Long Melford	Kentwell Hall Home Farm	Tour 13

Houses - open to the public

Horringer	Ickworth House	Tour 12
Haughley	Haughley Park	Tour 16
Lavenham	Little Hall	Tour 2
Long Melford	Melford Hall	Tour 13
Long Melford	Kentwell Hall	Tour 13
Otley	Otley Hall	Tour 3
Somerleyton	Somerleyton Hall	Tour 5

Information Centres

Bury St Edmunds	Angel Hill	Tour 12
Felixstowe	Leisure Centre	Tour 7
Hadleigh	Topplesfield Hall	Tour 2
Ipswich	Town Hall	Tour 1
Lavenham	Lady St	Tour 2
Lowestoft	The Pavilion	Tour 5
Newmarket	The Rookery	Tour 14
Southwold	Town Hall	Tour 9
Stowmarket	Wilkes Way	Tour 11
Sudbury	Town Hall	Tour 17

Market Days

Beccles	Friday	Tour 5
Brandon	Thursday & Saturday	Tour 15
Bury St Edmunds	Wednesday & Saturday	Tour 12
Framlingham	Saturday	Tour 4
Hadleigh	Friday & Saturday	Tour 2
Ipswich	Tuesday, Friday & Saturday	Tour 1
Lowestoft	Friday, Saturday & Sunday	Tour 5
Stowmarket	Thursday & Saturday	Tour 11
Sudbury	Thursday & Saturday	Tour 17

Museums

Beccles		Tour 5
Beccles	Printing Museum	Tour 5
Brandon	Heritage Centre	Tour 15
Bungay		Tour 10
Bury St Edmunds	Manor House Museum	Tour 12
Bury St Edmunds	Moyse's Hall Museum	Tour 12
Bury St Edmunds	Suffolk Regiment Museum	Tour 12
Bury St Edmunds	Market Cross Art Gallery	Tour 12
Carlton Colville	Transport Museum	Tour 5
Cavendish	Sue Ryder Foundation	Tour 13
Cotton	Mechanical Music Museum	Tour 16

Nature Reserves and Sanctuaries

Westleton	Minsmere Nature Reserve	Tour 9
West Stow	Country Park &	
	Anglo-Saxon Village	Tour 15

Police Stations

Aldeburgh	Leiston Rd	Tour 3
Beccles	London Rd	Tour 5
Bury St Edmunds	Raingate St	Tour 12
Eye	Victoria Rd	Tour 16
Felixstowe	High St	Tour 7
Hadleigh	High St	Tour 2
Haverhill	Swan Lane	Tour 13
Ipswich	Civic Drive	Tour 1
Leiston	King's Rd	Tour 3
Lowestoft	Old Nelson St	Tour 5
Mildenhall	Kingsway	Tour 15
Newmarket	Vicarage Rd	Tour 14
Southwold	Station Rd	Tour 9
Stowmarket	Violet Hill Rd	Tour 11
Sudbury	Acton Lane	Tour 17
Thetford	Norwich Rd	Tour 15
Woodbridge	Grundisburgh Rd	Tour 3

Railways

Mendlesham	Light Railway	Tour 6

Tours

Lowestoft	Fishing Industry Tour	Tour 5
Newmarket	Thoroughbred Tours	Tour 14
Sudbury	Vintage Coach Tours	Tour 17

Vineyards

Aldeburgh		Tour 3
Ashbocking	Juice & Cider centre	Tour 3
Bruisyard	Vineyard & Herb centre	Tour 9
Cavendish	Manor Vineyard	Tour 13
Framlingham	Shawsgate Vineyard	Tour 4
Hartest	Gifford's Hall	Tour 13
Ilketshall St Lawrence	The Cider Place	Tour 10
Mildenhall	Eros Vineyard	Tour 15
Stanton	Wyken Vineyards & Gardens	Tour 16
Stoke-by-Clare	Boyton Vineyard	Tour 13
Wissett	Wissett Wines	Tour 10

Holton	St Peter's windmill	Tour 5
Letheringham	Windmill & Gardens	Tour 4
Pakenham	Water Mill & Windmill	Tour 11
Saxtead Green	Post Mill	Tour 3
Sproughton	Mill & House	Tour 11
Thorington St	Mill	Tour 8
Thorpeness	The House in the Clouds	Tour 3
Woodbridge	Buttrums Mill	Tour 3
Woodbridge	Tide Mill	Tour 3

Other Places of Interest

Buildings, Monuments & other Constructions

Aldeburgh	Martello Tower	Tour 3
Aldeburgh	Alde House	Tour 3
Beccles	Roos Hall	Tour 5
Bradfield-St-Clare	Bradfield Woods	Tour 17
Brandon	Heritage centre	Tour 15
Bury St Edmunds	Gershom Parkington Collection of clocks & watches	Tour 12
Clare	Ancient House	Tour 13
Dunwich	Underwater Exploration	Tour 9
Felixstowe	Martello Tower	Tour 7
Felixstowe	Fort	Tour 7
Flatford	Bridge Cottage	Tour 8
Flatford	Willy Lott's House	Tour 8
Framlingham	2 Victorian Post Boxes	Tour 4
Framlingham	College	Tour 4
Grimes Graves	Flint mines	Tour 15
Hadleigh	Overall House	Tour 2
Haverhill	Ann of Cleaves House	Tour 13
Ipswich	Christchurch Mansion	Tour 1
Ipswich	Ancient House	Tour 1
Ipswich	Alton Waters	Tour 1
Ipswich	Pykenham's Gatehouse	Tour 1
Lavenham	Market Place	Tour 2
Lavenham	Angel Corner	Tour 2
Lavenham	Priory	Tour 2
Long Melford	Trinity Hospital	Tour 13
Moulton	Pack Horse Bridge & Ford	Tour 14
Newmarket	Jockey Club	Tour 14
Newmarket	Nell Gwynne's cottage	Tour 14
Orford	Dunwich Underwater Exploration	Tour 3
Oulton Broads	Boatworld shipbuilding	Tour 5

Sporting interests

Bicycles

Boating & Sailing

Cruises

Fishing

Clare	Tour 13
Oulton Broad	Tour 5
Sudbury	Tour 17

Golf

Aldeburgh	Aldeburgh Golf Club	Tour 3
Beccles	Wood Valley Golf Club	Tour 5
Bungay	Bungay & Waveney	Tour 10
Bury St Edmunds	Bury St Edmunds Golf Club	Tour 12
Carlton Colville	The Rookery	Tour 5
Cretingham	Cretingham Golf Course	Tour 3
Eye	Diss Golf Course, Stuston	Tour 16
Felixstowe	Felixstowe Ferry Golf Club	Tour 7
Flempton	Flempton Park Golf Club	Tour 15
Fornham St Martin	Fornham Park Golf Club	Tour 15
Gorleston-on-Sea	Gorleston Golf Club	Tour 5
Halesworth	St Helena Golf Club	Tour 5
Haverhill	Haverhill Golf Club	Tour 13
Ipswich	Ipswich Golf Club	Tour 1
Newmarket	Links Golf Club	Tour 14
Southwold		Tour 9
Stonham Aspal	Driving range	Tour 6
Stowmarket	Stowmarket Golf Club	Tour 11
Sudbury	Newton Green Golf Club	Tour 17
Thetford	Thetford Golf Club	Tour 15
Thorpeness	Thorpeness Golf Club & Hotel	Tour 3
Woodbridge	Woodbridge Golf Course	Tour 3

Horses & Horse Riding

Barnby	Riding school	Tour 5
Newmarket	Thoroughbred Tours	Tour 14
Newmarket	National Stud	Tour 14
Sudbury	Twinstead Riding Centre	Tour 17
Sudbury	High Banks	Tour 17
Wickham Market	Valley Farm Camargue Horses	Tour 4
Woodbridge	Equestrian Centre	Tour 3

INDEX OF TOWNS

OTHER TITLES BY LITTLE HILLS PRESS

DRIVING GUIDES

Australia's Central & Western Outback .... A$24.95
Australia's Northern Outback .... A$24.95
Australia's Eastern Outback .... A$24.95
Driving Guide to Britain - Norfolk .... A$11.95
Driving Guide to Britain - Suffolk .... A$11.95

LITTLE HILLS GUIDES

Australia .... A$19.95
Australia's Great Barrier Reef .... A$14.95
Bali .... A$11.95
California .... A$11.95
Cambodia .... A$14.95
Cuba .... A$16.95
Europe ... . A$14.95
Hawaii .... A$11.95
Hong Kong & Macau .... A$16.95
India .... A$ 9.95
Korea (nyp) .... A$14.95
New Zealand .... A$16.95
Outback Australia .... A$19.95
Singapore & Malaysia .... A$14.95
Tasmania .... A$14.95
Thailand .... A$11.95

POCKET GUIDE BOOKS

Brisbane & Gold Coast (nyp) .... A$ 9.95
London .... A$ 5.95
Moscow (nyp) .... A$ 9.95
Perth & Margaret River (nyp) .... A$ 9.95
Singapore .... A$ 5.95
Sydney (nyp) .... A$ 9.95

FOR ORDERS & ENQUIRIES CONTACT:-

LITTLE HILLS PRESS
11 /37-43 Alexander Street, Crows Nest. NSW 2065
Fax: (612) 9438-5762 Tel: (612) 9437-6995
Email: littlehills@peg.apc.org
Home Page: http://www.peg.apc.org/~littlehills